"JIM NUSSBAUM IS A REAl the opportunity to meet many Nussbaum is in the highest eche ......, ... five decades, has firmly cemented his place among the industry's all-time greats."

– Hal Krause,
Founder and CEO, American Salesmasters,
Founder and CEO, Crestcom International

"A 'must read' if you want to become a real estate agent of significance. Practical lessons shared by one of America's best."

– Robert Bohlen,
World's Number One Prudential Real Estate Agent for 10 Years

"As one of Denver's most successful real estate brokers with a storied career spanning 50 years, Jim Nussbaum is the perfect spokesman for the tried and true methods that lead to success. He shows why sales training and goal setting are invaluable in achieving our goals as sales people as well as our personal life objectives. I personally benefited from many of the people and examples outlined in this book and enjoyed refreshing my memory on the value of taking the advice found in these pages. Human nature has not changed much over the years and employing these basic principles are the keys successful people understand and endorse."

– Jack Box,
Regional Chairman, Newmark Knight Frank

"As I've reached a certain level of success in my life, building a legacy has become a major motivator to keep going through difficult times. Jim's book is the perfect roadmap for outlasting adversity, building a life of purpose and prosperity around the love for family, and making a positive personal and professional impact that will last for generations."

– Ford Saeks,
Hall of Fame Speaker and author of *Superpower!*

"Jim Nussbaum's memoir, *Significance: A Lifetime of Learning, Earning and Love,* illustrates how resilience and drive can propel someone with focus to success, even while overcoming unthinkable tragedies like terminal cancer and the loss of a child. This is a simple guide that, if followed, will impart a systematic textbook on how to turn lemons into lemonade and hard work into wealth."

– Gretchen Rosenberg,
President and CEO, Kentwood Real Estate

"I am so impressed that Jim is providing the Real Estate industry unprecedented access to his lifetime of knowledge, experience, and results. This most meticulously crafted and comprehensive examination of what is required to create and combine a successful career with a healthy and abundant life is truly in a class of its own."

– Gino Blefari,
CEO, Home Services of America,
Chairman, Berkshire Hathaway HomeServices

"Anyone new to Real Estate will receive a five-year head start by reading *Significance,* while experienced agents who suffer from a malignancy of over-information will appreciate how *Significance* stripped of excess verbiage provides a laserlike clarity on how to maximize human potential."

– Allan Dalton,
Former CEO, Realtor.com, CEO, Real Living Real Estate,
SVP, Berkshire Hathaway HomeServices

"I would encourage all to read *Significance* written by my long-time friend, Jim Nussbaum. I want to thank Jim for taking the time to share with all of us his personal journey over a long and accomplished career. Jim articulates many practically useful gems from his own life's experiences that all of us can benefit from."

– William B. Pauls

SIGNIFICANCE

A Lifetime of Learning, Earning and Love

JIM NUSSBAUM
CRS, GRI, SRES, CIPS, CDPE

This book is for informational purposes only and is not meant to constitute legal advice. Any person consulting these materials is solely responsible for implementation of this guidance as it relates to the particular matter for which the end user refers to these materials.

While every effort has been made to ensure the accuracy of the attributions of the content of this book, the author makes no claim to any third-party companies nor their content.

Published by Prime Concepts Group Press.

Design cover and composition by Prime Concepts Group, Inc.

Publisher's Catalogue-in-Publication LCCN: 2020920237

Print ISBN: 978-1-884667-34-3

eBook ISBN: 978-1-884667-36-7

DEDICATION

Eric, my son, I am dedicating this book to you. I want you to know that you lived a life that mattered and were a profound and lasting influence on my life and the lives of many other people. You are a constant reminder to me that one can live a life that matters just by "being" and not by the necessity of "doing."

TABLE OF CONTENTS

ACKNOWLEDGMENTS

GRATITUDE IS SO important to the smooth and proper functioning of real estate sales, and to any sales effort for that matter, that I have devoted a chapter to it in my book.

I am grateful to so many people for their encouraging and helpful comments and advice as I have embarked upon the journey of writing this book. It is virtually impossible for me to adequately thank everyone that has been there for me, sharing their thoughts with me and being so helpful, but I will try.

First and foremost, my wife, Mary Jean, has patiently endured my many years and long hours of selling real estate over fifty years; she faithfully had prepared for me many a late-night dinner after I arrived home from an evening listing appointment, and has given me the all-important perspective as she has read my many drafts of the manuscript. My children, Dan and Kate, have always been kind enough to give me their comments as well. My long-term friend from graduate school, Jim Gennrich, took his time on our family vacation together to review in detail my early manuscript and provided very helpful insights. One of my founding partners of The Kentwood Company, Roger Campbell, and his wife, Arna, gave me valuable input on the selection of the cover design for the book.

I owe a great debt of gratitude to Brian Buffini, Chairman and Founder of Buffini and Company and the author of his own best-selling book, *The Emigrant Edge*. Despite his extremely busy schedule, Brian has made time over several years to help me with input that has proven invaluable in my editing of the many drafts of my book. One of the top Realtors in the United States, Bob Bohlen, who has authored his own real estate book, *Clarity*, reviewed and edited my book on very short notice and provided some very helpful insights and suggestions. Larry Kendall, best-selling author of *Ninja Selling* and a very successful real estate trainer and seminar leader, read the draft of my book and made invaluable suggestions and comments. Brian, Bob and Larry also took the time to give me a written testimonial, as did seven other sales, marketing and real estate icons. A huge thank you to these 10 people!

In the course of hand-writing all the many drafts of my book, I used untold numbers of yellow, lined note pad sheets with scribbled notes and arrows going here, there and everywhere. Karen Porras, my private assistant for over 17 years, did a fantastic job of deciphering what I had written and transferring my notes to a computer PDF. Michealann Nofzinger also was a great help in assisting with the typing and compilation of the final versions.

Many other colleagues and individuals have encouraged me and helped me with their advice over the several years that it has taken me to write this book, and I simply and humbly say a most sincere and heartfelt thank you to all of them.

INTRODUCTION

"The doctor told me I had terminal cancer, and I thought I was going to die!"

Fortunately, through the grace of God, many prayers, and against all odds, I experienced a cure and the doctor was wrong! However, the stress of not knowing whether I was going to live or die was very traumatic and posed a real challenge to my mental sanity, especially since all this occurred right at the time that I was just starting my business career.

Another profoundly stressful challenge occurred to me and my wife after I was in residential real estate sales for only about two years. Our newly-adopted, infant son, Eric, suddenly developed a high fever, fell into a deep coma, and stayed in that coma until he passed away on Valentine's Day weekend fourteen years later.

Very few if any of us leave this earth without being exposed to one or more life-challenging, emotional experiences like the two that I faced, and those experiences can test the very fiber of our being. It was tough, but I learned how to sell real estate successfully in spite of my two challenges. I then decided to write this book and share how I dealt with these challenges in the hope that my sharing will help you better handle any serious roadblocks that rear their ugly heads in your life as you pursue your real estate sales career.

Whether you are new to the real estate sales business and are full of excitement as you start out "brand new" in your sales career, or if you have been selling real estate for some time and have strayed from the basic success principles that gave you some measure of success, and are now experiencing a loss of enthusiasm, slipping into the condition I call "drift" and loss of focus, I am excited to walk both of you through, step by step, what I did from start to finish over my fifty-plus-year real estate sales career to close more than 2,800 transactions and $1.3 Billion in sales. I will show you in detail what I did to move from a Survival mode to a Stability mode, to a Success mode and finally to a Significance mode. I will explain the characteristics, challenges and opportunities in each of these four modes or levels and how I dealt with them as I grew increasingly proficient in my real estate sales career. I am excited that you are joining me on this journey. Let's begin!

1.

How I Managed Adversity

I Am Diagnosed With Terminal Cancer

AS I MENTIONED in the Introduction, I had two major personal challenges that I experienced early in my business and sales career. The first was my diagnosis of a terminal cancer.

After I earned my Master's Degree in Business Administration/Marketing (MBA) from the University of Wisconsin, Madison, Wisconsin, I joined the General Electric Corporation (GE) on its MBA training program.

About the time I joined GE, I noticed swollen lymph nodes in the left side of my neck; initially I did not think much of it, but eventually I thought I should get them checked out. When I was home for the holidays in December, 1965, the doctors recommended a biopsy. I will never forget the doctor calling my dad and me into a small office in the corner of the hospital and saying, "My grandfather had this and lived a long time." I remember saying, "What do

I have, is it cancer?" The doctor said it was, and the diagnosis was lympho-sarcoma. The prognosis was not good. I staggered out of the office thinking, "Here I am with my whole life ahead of me and this happens."

That evening I was on a date with my then-girlfriend, Mary Jean, and I really did not know what to say. She was staying at her friend's home in Appleton, Wisconsin, my hometown. I will never forget driving her home that evening to her friend's home which was located at the end of a cul-de-sac. I remember thinking, "Well, as soon as I tell her that will be the end of it for us. Why would she want to continue going out with a guy who is apparently terminally ill?" I put my arms around her and told her, fully thinking she would just say goodbye, go into the house, and that would be that. Well, to my surprise and relief, she threw her arms around me and said, "Let's go for it!" That was a defining moment in my life and gave me the courage to press on, secure in the fact that Mary Jean was marching right alongside me!

I continued to work with GE on its training program, transferring to five divisions of the company in one year. After leaving the training program I joined GE's educational affiliate, General Learning Corporation, working in Washington, D.C. and New York City. Mary Jean and I got married on December 31, 1966, and I can't tell you how helpful it was to have her in my cheering section! The doctors were treating my condition with a powerful drug called Cytoxan. I would be less than truthful if I said I was not scared. I really was! I even went to the Mayo Clinic in Rochester, Minnesota, with all my records, and they unfortunately confirmed the original diagnosis.

I came from a very religious Roman Catholic family and we all had a deep faith in God that was instilled within us by our parents. I promised God that I would say a rosary every day if he would grant me a cure. To this day I carry my rosary with me in my pocket and it is on my bedside table at night. I brush a relic of Saint Frances Xavier Cabrini over the areas of my body where lymph nodes are prevalent every evening before retiring, along with some blessed holy water from Lourdes, France. To some this may seem like overkill or even verging upon the superstitious. But to me it has given me the strength to face each day while doing my everyday work and praying that I would be granted a cure.

By the grace of God I have been fortunate to be cancer-free for over 50 years! Nevertheless, I was surprised, dismayed and frightened to receive a call from my family care physician on the afternoon of June 19, 2020, telling me that the sonogram of my kidneys revealed a malignant growth in my right kidney!

Obviously, I was shocked to hear this, but the decision was made to remove the entire kidney by surgery to make sure the entire cancerous growth was removed. Subsequent pathology tests fortunately showed no cancer whatsoever beyond that kidney, and I was told that no radiation or chemotherapy would be needed! And of course, I have my left kidney that is functioning fine!

All this had happened within the last year, and as I reflect on what has taken place, my immediate reaction has been one of intense relief and gratitude for a diagnosis that was the best news I could possibly have hoped for. I find myself also feeling grateful for the exceptional care and concern shown to me by the doctors, nurses and other medical staff that attended to me. I am a very fortunate individual!

Our Infant Adopted Son, Eric, Falls Into a 14-Year Coma and Dies

In addition to my cancer diagnosis, a second big obstacle to moving forward with my business career and my life in general was our infant adopted son, Eric, suddenly falling into a deep coma and remaining in that coma for 14 years before he passed away on the day after Valentine's Day.

By way of background, when my wife and I found out that we could not naturally have children we explored the possibility of adoption. We applied to Arapahoe County, Colorado, filled out a lot of paperwork, met with social workers, and then waited excitedly for a phone call. It was more than a year before we heard that a baby was available from Montrose County, Colorado. We flew to Montrose and picked up little Eric. He was a cute, blond-haired and blue-eyed, 4¾ month-old little boy; we were so excited!

We were enjoying all the fun of having a new addition to our family, and the good news was Eric was beyond the age where he would keep us up nights, and he was a joy to behold.

One day when Eric was about 11 months old I happened to come home at the same time that an ambulance was in front of our home. I ran inside to find the attendant working on our son, who was convulsing. He finally stopped convulsing and we went to the emergency room, where they felt the convulsions were being caused by a high fever. They gave Eric some Tylenol and sent us home for the evening.

The next morning I awoke early to the sound of my wife bathing little Eric in the bathtub full of lukewarm water, trying to cool him off (his high fever of 104 degrees was back!). We were just a young couple at this time, and we decided we better quickly take Eric to our pediatrician's office. We sat there for over an hour in the waiting room before he was examined; having seen our son, the doctor said we should take Eric to the emergency room immediately.

The trip to the emergency room at the hospital started a new, horrible chapter in our life. We were sitting in the waiting room while two doctors examined Eric. While in that room we suddenly saw quite a few white-coated personnel running from all directions and I asked my wife, a Registered Nurse, what was happening. She said the hospital was calling a "code blue", which meant a patient's heart had stopped. Well, that "code blue" patient was our little Eric! While undergoing a spinal tap to check for spinal meningitis, Eric's heart stopped. Being draped, the medical personnel didn't realize right away that his heart had stopped, and he slipped into a deep coma from which he never recovered.

We obviously were devastated, crushed, angry and mad! Here we were, not able to have kids, wanting them so badly, and then this happens!

Mary Jean and I spent most of that summer's months in Denver's Children's Hospital. We always held out hope that little Eric might come out of the coma, but then the doctors performed a test called a pneumoencephalogram that would give us a definitive prognosis for Eric's potential for recovery. We were crushed by the news that Eric's brain had shrunk drastically from the loss of oxygen; no hope now existed, and he would be profoundly disabled and remain comatose for the rest of his life.

We took Eric home with us just to see if we could handle the situation but he was dead weight, and Mary Jean started crying realizing that we just could not adequately take care of him at home. He was being fed through a tube inserted in his stomach, was blind, his sense of hearing was minimal to non-existent, and he was totally paralyzed.

We did some research and found Ridge Home, a Colorado state facility that provided a group home for disabled children like our Eric. By a strange twist of fate, the gentleman who was my manager with American Salesmasters, my employer after GE, had a daughter at Ridge, and he and his wife and Mary Jean and I became even closer because of our sharing of a common tragedy.

Mary Jean and I subsequently adopted two more children, Dan and Kate, and the four of us would go out frequently to Ridge Home to see Eric. We would have parties for the kids there on the various holidays. It is quite an experience to see 50-100 profoundly disabled children and adults in a group setting! Mary Jean and I will never forget the smiles and the love emanating from the aides that worked there. They were probably earning at best a minimum wage, but the love and care that they showed to those mal-formed, severely disabled human beings was something that will stay with us forever. It reminded me of the saying from the bible: "Whatever you do to the least of my brethren, that you do unto me."

We tried to keep a positive mental attitude about the whole situation, but it was very difficult. We had a deep sense of emptiness, of being abandoned, and with no family in town we felt very alone.

Eric mercifully died Valentine's Day weekend when he was 15 years old, having been in a coma for 14 years! Of course, our Catholic faith was being tested. Our pediatrician told us that a tragedy like this either blows your marriage apart or brings you much closer together as a couple; fortunately, our experience was the latter, not the former.

As a result of this experience we have become more tolerant of people and more appreciative of our good health. We also appreciate the little things in life much more, like a beautiful day, the blue sky, and the birds chirping in the trees. We are grateful for what we have, and we certainly will never take our health for granted!

2.

How I Set the Foundation

Establishing My Systems for Goal-Setting

IN JANUARY, 1970, I found myself increasingly bored with my General Learning Corporation, salaried job and was approached by a firm actually headquartered in Denver named American Salesmasters (A/S), the job being to sell tickets to a Sales Congress attended by approximately 2,500 people and to be held in Carnegie Hall in New York City in June of that year. We had four internationally known sales trainers and motivational speakers come to speak at our Congress. My job was to cold call any company in New York City that had a sales force and get an appointment with the sales manager to allow one of us to come back at their next sales meeting and give them a sample presentation of the main program. Our goal was to sell as many tickets as possible to the upcoming Congress.

Parenthetically, whenever my real estate sales get a little slow and I have bumps in the road, I remind myself that I did cold calling successfully in New York City and that if I could sell there, I hopefully could sell anywhere! I rubbed shoulders with some of the greatest people in the sales motivational and training industry, people like Dr. Norman Vincent Peale, J. Douglas Edwards, Bob Richards, and Dr. Maxwell Maltz.

While working with Salesmasters, I was introduced to a recording by the late Earl Nightingale titled *The Strangest Secret.* In that recording Mr. Nightingale gave some statistics that I will never forget. He said that if you take 100 people in the United States at age 25 and follow them through life to age 65, the following will be their status: 36 will be dead, one will be rich, four will be financially independent, five will still be working, and 54 will be broke, i.e., dependent on some outside source for their existence. And this situation exists in the richest country on the face of the earth! These figures are essentially still accurate unfortunately even today, and hearing them put the fear of God in me.

I decided right then and there that I was not going to be in the group of 54, but rather in the group of five that were rich or financially independent. I then had to decide how I would accomplish that goal. My studies further led me to read a book by Napoleon Hill called *Think and Grow Rich.* In his book Mr. Hill states that to be successful we need to set up goals, and those goals need the following characteristics in order to be effective: they must be (1) realistic; (2) specific; (3) a definite date must be established for their fulfillment and (4) a plan set up to achieve those goals. They must be (5) written and then repeated over and over until they become a part of you. One then must develop (6) a sincere desire to achieve the goals and a "dogged determination" to follow through on the plan to achieve them regardless of circumstances, obstacles, criticism or what other people say, think or do.

I still have the 3" x 5" cards that my wife and I jointly filled out in March, 1970, detailing our goals. Establishing those goals and reading them every day became another defining chapter in our lives! As I got started in my career, I applied those goals and principles to real estate.

We had a very successful Sales Congress that first half of 1970 in New York City, and then Salesmasters asked me if I would move to the Denver area to sell tickets to their next program. Mary Jean and I had some trepidation about moving across the country, especially given my medical condition, but we decided to go for it, and we loaded all our possessions in a small U-Haul trailer, attached that trailer to our 1965 Chevrolet Impala, and drove west.

A/S had asked me to take over the Pueblo and Colorado Springs, Colorado markets and sell tickets in those cities for the program to be held in late 1970 in Denver. Again, I was attempting to get appointments for myself or for one of my colleagues to come to the client's next sales meeting to give a sample of the main program and sell tickets to it.

A/S at that time had approximately 85 salespeople throughout the United States. I was number 1 or 2 in the country in ticket sales out of all those salespeople and I made only about $7,500 annualized for that year! In fact, my wife, Mary Jean, was making more than I was working as a Registered Nurse at Saint Luke's Hospital!

She would take the bus west down Colfax Avenue to Pearl Street in full white nurse's uniform and walk the several blocks north to the hospital. It was then that I had another defining moment like the one I mentioned earlier, when my wife supported me when I told her about my cancer.

I said "I am going to get paid what I am worth!" I quit A/S, took and passed my real estate examination, got my real estate license, and started selling real estate in December of that year in Aurora, Colorado.

Since goals are so very critical to our success, early on I devoured every book and piece of information that I could find on goal-setting. I owe a huge debt of gratitude to my good friend, Brian Buffini, Buffini and Company, who taught me the importance of having goals properly balanced in each of the five broad areas of life, namely **Spiritual, Family, Financial, Business and Personal**. The graphic presentation of these areas is arranged in a circular format, and the circles are intertwined to show that they all work together. The dictionary defines balance as "being harmonious in proper arrangement or stability; things being in proportion; a state of equilibrium or to keep steady." If one of the circular areas is exaggerated and no longer circular, it is oblong, and in that condition, like the flat tires on a car, will not move around smoothly, but will suffer and strain to move at all. The necessary harmony of the circles working together is broken and compromised.

This is like me when I was working so hard in the early years of my career to achieve in the **Business** and **Financial** areas. Those circles in my life moved with great difficulty; life was oftentimes out of control for me, and I was not getting enough sleep, was not exercising enough, and felt like I was on a giant treadmill with no end in sight. I owe many thanks to Brian for giving me the framework within which to establish my goal-setting and to achieve more personal balance in the five goal areas.

Brian speaks of the Key to Success being threefold: (1) establish your values, i.e., what you believe (2) create your goals, i.e., what you want and (3) outline your vision, i.e., where you want to go. Goals are the end to which all effort is directed and need to be written; be very specific; have deadlines and milestones; be connected to your gifts and talents; be measured as you progress; be constant; re-evaluated as your circumstances in life change, and provide the basis for rewarding yourself when a goal is achieved, i.e., celebrate its achievement! The payoff here is stated so eloquently by the great sales motivational pioneer, Paul Meyer, when he says, "whatever you vividly imagine, ardently desire, sincerely believe, and enthusiastically act upon ... must inevitably come to pass!" As Mahatma Gandhi so well puts it, "a man is but a product of his thought. What he thinks he becomes."

I have known a fair number of associates, colleagues, and friends, as well as myself, who do not take time to celebrate an achievement. The Good Lord wants us to be joyful and we should never forget that. In other words, all work and no play is not what He had planned for us. I will make some additional comments on this aspect of play at the end of this chapter.

I would now like to cover the Buffini circle areas in more detail as they have worked in my life.

Spiritual

1.   Love the Lord your God with your whole heart and soul and with all your mind, and your neighbor as yourself (Matthew 22:37).

     The key here is to love yourself first before you can fully and completely love others! This has always been difficult for me to accomplish. I would tend to focus on what I did wrong rather than focus on the many things I did right. Someone once told me something that has been very helpful to me in this regard, namely, "Beyond a reasonable discipline, be good to yourself!"

2.   A book that has helped me very much with this concept of loving myself is Rabbi Harold S. Kushner's book, *How Good Do We Have to Be?* In this book Rabbi Kushner is quoted as saying: "It is the notion that we were supposed to be perfect, and that we could expect others to be perfect because we need them to be, that leaves us feeling constantly guilty and perpetually disappointed. But the more I, as a clergyman dealt with people's problems and the more I, as a husband, son, father, brother, and friend

learned to look at my own life honestly, the more convinced I became that a lot of misery could be traced to this one mistaken notion: we need to be perfect for people to love us and we forfeit that love if we ever fall short of perfection."

I certainly have had issues with the idea that I had to be perfect in order to be loved. Being the oldest of five children, I was always the child called upon to give the example. I can remember my parents telling me over and over to "stand tall with your shoulders pushed back!" Of course, growing up in my era, parents had difficulty expressing love and giving compliments. So, since I had not experienced direct compliments and love, it was hard for me to give compliments, affection, and love.

3. Another influence on my journey away from having to be perfect are the thoughts contained in Philip Yancy's book, *What's So Amazing About Grace?* Essentially, Yancy says God loves us just the way we are, accepts us for what we are, and forgives us. From his book, I learned that I need to cut myself some slack, first by giving myself some grace, and by doing so I can then do the best possible job in my interactions with others.

4. I found that I could be more productive with less stress if I learned to meditate. In this regard I found Father Thomas Keating's contemplative prayer movement to be very helpful. His book, *Open Mind Open Heart*, is well worth reading and has helped me tremendously.

5. I learned to work as little as possible on Sunday, the Sabbath, because it is a day of rest. Even the good Lord rested one day, and I believe we should emulate Him in this regard.

Finally, I found that if I kept my priorities in focus my days went so much better. A really helpful saying for me here is what my wife shared with me several years ago, namely, "You would not worry so much about what people think about you if you realize how seldom they think about you." When I tend to lose perspective and get wrapped up in what other people say or do as it might relate to me, I remember this quote and it has been very helpful for me.

Family

Perspective-wise, a recent study showed that many middle-class kids will spend approximately 54 hours/ week in front of the TV! The people running the study asked the dad how much time he spent with his kids each day. The dad estimated that it was almost 40 minutes, but the study showed that the actual time was 37.7 seconds!! When the study asked the kids which they preferred, TV or dad, 92 percent said they preferred the time with dad! So, we dads need to be more attentive to our kids!

I was very influenced by this study, and throughout my real estate career I tried to spend quality time with my kids. However, I found that I had to really work at carving out that quality time. I came up with an effective technique where I set up a "date night," a one-on-one with each of my children; we would do fun things like go to a movie, get a Dairy Queen "Blizzard," or take my daughter to the circus.

By the way, my daughter is 43, and we really enjoyed our "one-on-one" going to the Ringling Brothers Circus, even though it is no longer in business. You are never too old to keep good memories alive!

One of the activities I will always remember is the special family times associated with our membership in the Ports-of-Call Travel Club. This was a club headquartered adjacent to the grounds of the old Stapleton Airport in Denver, Colorado. Through this club we would sign up for five-day fun trips to destinations in popular vacation places like Mexico and the Caribbean. Having signed up for these trips and having paid for them, we went regardless, and they provided me and my family with incredibly valuable and meaningful family time together.

A significant help for me to keep my family time in sharp focus was reading frequently from the plaque that I have hanging in my study at home that contains the words to the song, "Cats In The Cradle" by Harry Chapin and Sandra Chapin.

My child arrived just the other day
He came to the world in the usual way
But there were planes to catch, and bills to pay
He learned to walk while I was away
And he was talking 'fore I knew it, and as he grew
He'd say, "I'm gonna be like you, dad
You know I'm gonna be like you."

And the cat's in the cradle and the silver spoon
Little boy blue and the man in the moon
"When you coming home, dad?" "I don't know when
But we'll get together then
You know we'll have a good time then."

My son turned ten just the other day
He said, "Thanks for the ball, dad; come on, let's play
Can you teach me to throw?"
I said, "Not today, I got a lot to do."
He said, "That's okay."
And he walked away, but his smile never dimmed
And said, "I'm gonna be like him, yeah
You know I'm gonna be like him."

And the cat's in the cradle and the silver spoon
Little boy blue and the man in the moon
"When you coming home, dad?" "I don't know when
But we'll get together then
You know we'll have a good time then."

Well, he came from college just the other day
So much like a man, I just had to say
"Son, I'm proud of you. Can you sit for a while?"
He shook his head, and he said with a smile
"What I'd really like, dad, is to borrow the car keys
See you later; can I have them please?"

And the cat's in the cradle and the silver spoon
Little boy blue and the man in the moon
"When you coming home, son?" "I don't know when
But we'll get together then, dad

You know we'll have a good time then."

I've long since retired, and my son's moved away
I called him up just the other day
I said, "I'd like to see you if you don't mind."
He said, "I'd love to, dad, if I could find the time
You see, my new job's a hassle, and the kid's got the flu
But it's sure nice talking to you, dad
It's been sure nice talking to you."
And as I hung up the phone, it occurred to me
He'd grown up just like me
My boy was just like me

And the cat's in the cradle and the silver spoon
Little boy blue and the man in the moon
"When you coming home, son?" "I don't know when
But we'll get together then, dad
We're gonna have a good time then."

It haunted me that those words could someday come true
for my relationship with my kids! In other words, I worked
hard to ensure that my kids liked spending time with my
wife and me, and that they felt ok about taking the time
to be with us.

Another poem, author unknown, that has stayed with me
over the years is entitled "What Shall You Give To One Small
Boy?"

What shall you give to one small boy?
A football game, a windup toy?
A picture book, a puzzle pack, a train

That runs on a curving track? No, there's
plenty of time for such things yet.
Give him a day for his very own, just
one small day and his dad alone. A
Walk in the woods, a romp in the park,
a fishing trip from dawn to dark.
And the gift that only you can,
the companionship of his old man.
Games are outgrown and toys decay,
But he'll never forget if you give him a day.

These two pieces of work have always been with me in my home office as a continual reminder of the importance of quality time to be spent with my kids. I have learned to give my kids unconditional love and not to compare them with any of their friends. (I will be covering the challenges of "comparison" in a later chapter.) When all is said and done, kids need to be encouraged; and what they really need to hear is that we love them and are proud of them. As someone put it recently, two things we give our kids are roots, and the other is wings. We have to ground them with the basic principles and tenets of life, but then we have to let them fly, so to speak, even if upon occasion we see them coming down for a crash landing!

Business

As I mentioned in Chapter 1, my wife, Mary Jean, and I adopted our first child, Eric, and he fell into a deep coma at 11 months of age and stayed in that coma until he died 14 years later on Valentine's Day weekend.

Looking back, I believe that traumatic experience caused me to dive into my work, probably to keep my sanity with the grief I was experiencing. Up until that time I had enjoyed my work but was not addicted to it, as I verged on being after Eric's unfortunate experience. Were it not for a very understanding wife, our marriage might not have made it.

So I learned that we need to be careful to keep balance in our lives. We all know how difficult it is to achieve this goal of balance because of the extremes in our business, e.g., closings, no closings, buyers, no buyers, listings, no listings, and the like.

What helped my wife and me were many things, and one of the most helpful was the Dr. Fred Grosse Mentoring Group that we belonged to, comprised of six to seven top-producing Realtor couples from around the country. The group was headed by Dr. Fred Grosse, a very accomplished real estate business consultant and life coach. We Realtor couples would meet at different locations around the country every three months. Dr. Grosse had many worthwhile suggestions and comments that I use to this day. One that I will always remember is "we work to fund life." He also stressed the importance of engaging in "Dollar-Productive Activities". I will cover this in more detail in the chapter on Time Management, and I have included its chart in the Appendix.

From Dr. Grosse I learned the importance of coaching and holding myself accountable for my actions and activities. I found I was much more productive when I had someone to be accountable to between and after mentoring sessions. Bob Bohlen, whom I mentioned in the Acknowledgments and who wrote the excellent book called *Clarity*, also emphasizes the need to have someone to be accountable to in order to ensure that they reach their goals.

I also learned that you can't please everyone! Sometimes circumstances will occur over which you have no control, and the listing and/or the buyer will go to a competitor. I remember a situation where I was undoubtedly superior in every way to my competitor but I lost the listing. I was devastated but later found out that it was a divorce situation and the woman said I reminded her of her ex-husband! Well you can't change your basic looks, and once I learned this was the reason for the loss of the listing, I felt much better.

For years, again based on Brian Buffini's teaching, I separated my clients into A+, A, B and C clients. Obviously, I focused on the A+ and A clients, people who like you and will be very apt to refer you. I also kept in touch with my clients on a systematic basis; at each closing I would get their birth dates and then my teammate would enter those dates into my contact management program. When the date would come up, I would call the person, wishing them a happy birthday, asking them how they and their family were doing, and then at the same time asking for referrals. At this point I always remembered the biblical basis for prospecting, which is "ask and you shall receive", "seek and ye shall find" and "knock and it shall be opened unto you." In other words, if it is good enough for the good Lord, it is good enough for me.

Also, I tend to be quite serious and take things pretty seriously. I have learned to not be too intense and serious and to laugh more often! I try and keep my business in proper perspective. Our clients have their own lives to live and aren't always thinking about us and whether or not we need another listing. This is not a haughty or thoughtless process; it is just a reality of life and this realization has really helped me!

Financial

Another Defining Moment: When I was in the Army and before getting into real estate, I had a "defining moment" relating to lack of money. I was stationed at Fort Campbell, Kentucky, and really wanted to get to Nashville, Tennessee, to see the Grand Ole Opry. I had no money and was not sure how many more weekends I would have to travel to Nashville to see that building before being shipped to another base location. So I dressed in my Army uniform to hopefully enhance my ability to get a ride and hitchhiked my way to Nashville from Fort Campbell. I got to Nashville and at that time the Opry building was on a side street and was relatively small. I walked up the steps, got to the front door, and told the ticket-taker that I did not have enough money to buy a ticket and was not sure if I would ever be able to come back, but would he be so kind as to just let me step inside briefly so that I could say that I had been in the Grand Ole Opry building; the ticket-taker would not allow me to go in. Then and there I vowed to myself that "I WILL NEVER BE THIS POOR AGAIN!"

I mention this story to emphasize that probably all of us have had several defining moments in our lives that in the long run prove to have been blessings in disguise.

- **Budget:** I found it very important to have a budget so my wife and I knew where we were with our finances. When I was with my first real estate company I was reasonably happy, but that firm had no pension program for its salespeople. Four of my fellow colleagues and I determined that because we were on straight commission, we would have only a limited number of years to work so hard at our current pace, and we really needed a retirement program into which we could funnel retirement dollars. We hired a sharp attorney to set such a program up for us, and it was one of the best things we ever did for ourselves. I cover this in more detail under the chapter on founding and selling my real estate company.

- **Financial Advisor:** I believe it is very important to have a competent financial advisor. I met my financial advisor over 40 years ago. Initially he helped with our income tax returns, and then when we had accumulated a reasonable amount of savings, we had him invest those excess dollars for us. He and his son are still our investment counselors to this day, and they set up managed accounts and oversee them for us. They receive a fee based on the dollar amount of investments managed and are not commission-based. I highly recommend that all individuals, including real estate salespeople, employ a financial advisor to help with the management of their assets.

You obviously have to trust the advisor. We continue to meet with our advisors every quarter, and they give us a status report on the performance of our asset categories in the financial markets. After I felt that our advisors were doing a good job, we turned over the entire portfolio to them. This can be hard to do, but I determined early on that I was better off using my time and energy to sell real estate, and let the advisors manage the dollar investment amounts that we had accumulated.

- **Monthly Investments:** Early on I also decided that my wife and I would live on 90 percent of our income, and we would religiously invest the other 10 percent. Referring back to the Earl Nightingale recording referenced earlier in this chapter and reiterated for emphasis here, 54 people out of 100 are broke after working 40 years from age 25 to age 65! I certainly did not want to be in that group of 54, but rather in the group where one will be rich and four will be financially independent.

- **Health and disability insurance:** I thought it very important to get this insurance. Being on straight commission, I could earn a good income as long as I was healthy; but if I became ill or otherwise incapacitated, I might have little or no income.

- **Will:** it surprised me to learn that over half of all United States families/individuals do not have a will! In my opinion, you must have a will, and if you do not, most of your estate and assets will unfortunately go directly to Uncle Sam upon your death.

Personal

Joe Ehrmann was a standout football player for the Baltimore Colts. He has been a pastor of a large church and speaks about the disfunction between a father and his son, and between a mother and her daughter.

I start with this discussion under the **Personal** section of goals because I believe it is so central to personal growth. Joe believes that three "lies" exist for a son, and he relates them to (1) the ball field; (2) the bedroom; and (3) the billfold (board room). He believes that boys feel they need to excel in sports, i.e., in athletic ability, size, and strength. They need to "excel" in the bedroom, i.e., sexual conquest, and excel in economic success. Joe believes boys to a greater or lesser degree are engaged as they grow up in a life-and-death struggle to validate their masculinity. Many of the boys that Joe coached were commonly found to have a dysfunctional relationship with their fathers, or in fact did not have a father figure at all but were raised by others. The two main questions of these boys were: (1) Who am I? (2) Who will love me?

On a personal note, and the reason Joe's statements resonate so vividly for me, was that I am the oldest of five kids, and my dad was typical of his era where he was struggling to be a provider, but was not a warm fuzzy guy who would grab you in his arms and say, "I love you." So, I knew rationally that he loved me, but had no tangible, emotional proof. I was attending the University of Wisconsin in Madison, Wisconsin about 110 miles from my hometown of Appleton, and one day I called dad and asked him if I could drive up and meet him at a bar on the outskirts of Appleton. He said fine, but I am sure he was wondering what was going on? Anyway, I met him and just asked him one simple question, namely "Do you love me?" Of course he said he did, and to this day I'm so glad I made that trip and asked that question. This is why from a personal point of view Joe's comments are so insightful and meaningful to me and gave me a better understanding of his comments and concerns.

Joe also speaks to the "lies" that society foists upon the girls in families. Society stresses (1) body type and size; (2) beauty, and the media defines what beauty really is and (3) belongings, i.e., the clothes a girl wears.

I just found Joe's analysis based upon his personal experiences to be very insightful and helpful to young boys and girls, as well as to myself, trying to figure out who they are and what they are going to do with their life.

- **Brisk Walking.** One hour per day. My wife and I walk approximately three miles per day at least 4-5 days a week, and I also work out with a personal trainer once a week. My wife has participated in a "gentle yoga" class once a week. The general consensus of medical experts is that the brisk walking routine provides a minimum amount of exercise to achieve maximum core strength and heart health.

- **Family Internist Doctor.** It almost goes without saying but it is so important to have a family doctor. My wife and I have always carefully chosen him or her. We have an annual physical and set up the appointment one year in advance for the following year. Surprisingly, I have talked to many people who do not have such a doctor in place, or if they do, they choose him or her almost exclusively based on that doctor's office proximity to their personal residence. This convenience factor is fine, but the doctor should be chosen primarily based upon his or her personal referrals from patients and from one's own research. Additionally, eye, dental and other appointments should be scheduled at the start of the year. Obviously, the old adage that "an ounce of prevention is worth a pound of cure" applies here for sure, and an even older adage goes back to the Greek physician, Hippocrates, in 400 BC, who said "Let food be thy medicine and medicine be thy food."

Along this same line of reasoning, I would like to share with you here some food and drink suggestions that have served me well over the years.

- **Drink** at least eight 8-ounce glasses of water each day.

- **Minimize intake** of white flour products, including bread, pasta, and pastries.

- **Red Meat** - Many nutritionists recommend minimizing our intake of red meat. However, if I want to eat red meat I focus on bison (buffalo). Here are the comparative facts from the United States Department of Agriculture (USDA) for 100 grams of ground meat (4 ounce portion):

	Bison	Beef	Pork	Chicken
Fat	2.429 g	9.28 g	9.66 g	7.41 g
Calories	143	211	212	190
Cholesterol	82 mg	86 mg	86 mg	89 mg

- **Avoid sugar.** Americans consume 11.4 pounds of sugar per person per month, or 137 pounds per person per year! Dr. Joel Fuhrman, a noted health clinician and author of *Fast Food Genocide*, says that this figure is actually higher, approximately 170 pounds per person per year! We also consume approximately 25 pounds of candy per person a year! A can of regular Pepsi has 12 teaspoons of sugar. No wonder we have an epidemic of type 2 diabetes in the United States!

- **Get more sleep.** In her book, *The Sleep Revolution*, Arianna Huffington says that more than 40 percent of Americans get less than the recommended minimum seven hours of sleep per night, and sleep deprivation is linked with increased risks of diabetes, heart attack, stroke, cancer, obesity, and Alzheimer's. She states as a fact that (page 108) 24 hours without sleep is the equivalent of a blood alcohol level of 0.1 percent – at which point you are more than legally drunk!

Arianna keeps a quote from Ralph Waldo Emerson by her bed that helps calm her mind: "Finish every day and be done with it... you have done what you could – some blunders and absurdities no doubt crept in, forget them as fast as you can, tomorrow is a new day. You shall begin it well and with serenity, and with too high a spirit to be encumbered with your old nonsense."

And finally, she quotes no less a financial guru than Warren Buffett who, in his 2008 letter to shareholders of Berkshire Hathaway, was quoted as saying "When forced to choose, I will not trade even a night's sleep for the chance of extra profit."

As a final perspective and as I alluded to earlier in this chapter, it is extremely important to have clearly defined goals and to work diligently toward achieving those goals. However, as Stuart Brown, M.D., states on page 115 of his ground-breaking book, simply called *Play*, "Goals are good, but overly rigid pursuit of those goals can inhibit growth and understanding."

Brown further defines play (page 60) as "all absorbing, apparently purposeless activity that provides enjoyment and a suspension of self-consciousness and sense of time."

In all my goal-setting activities I have always felt that I need to be purposeful and concerned about utilizing my time effectively. Of course, this is important, but Dr. Brown's comments have given me the perspective that I need periodically.

Also, I have always been very serious about my work and goal-achievement activities. Dr. Brown has taught me the importance of cutting myself some slack in my everyday activities. Toward that goal, he shows a picture of Albert Einstein smiling and riding a bike, and further references a very serious board member (page 50) who had his own play epiphany where he found himself alone on the beach and allowed himself to skip. He quotes the board member as follows: "I myself have often had the urge to skip when at the beach but thought people would think I was crazy. Regardless, I decided to do so one day; it was fun, and no one laughed at me. In fact, I did not really care if they did or not!"

Finally, Dr. Brown quotes the famous James Michener in his autobiography as follows:

"The master in the art of living makes little distinction between his work and his play, his labor and his leisure, his mind and his body, his information and his recreation, his love and his religion. He hardly knows which is which. He simply pursues his vision of excellence at whatever he does, leaving others to decide whether he is working or playing. To him he's always doing both."

So goals are important, but so is the apparently purposeless activity called "play!" It is almost an oxymoron that I am working hard to play more often. As Mahatma Gandhi says, "There is more to life than increasing its speed." Robert Louis Stevenson said, "To be what we are and to become what we are capable of becoming, is the only end of life. When we put our faith in others, we help them reach their potential – we become an important relationship in their lives – and they in ours."

How I Got Started in Selling Real Estate

Every one of us, myself included, has a weakness, and in fact it can be our greatest weakness, and that is giving up in different areas of our life at different times; often we give up at the very time that we are so close to succeeding. For those of you who are new to the business and just starting out, it is a challenge not to give up before even getting started. The thought goes through our head "I am new to the business, I know very few people, and I am afraid I am going to fail."

The very fact of fearing failure can be a self-fulfilling prophecy. What helped me when I was starting out and had these self-doubts was to say to myself, focusing on a Realtor who was successful, "Well, he (or she) is a nice person, but is no better in real estate sales than I am. I have just as much right to be successful as does that person." I kept this focus in front of me all the time as I got started in real estate. I kept saying to myself "If he can do it so can I; he is no better than I am."

So here is what worked for me in getting started in real estate on my way to a higher measure of success. By the way, much of this information will be good review for the second of the two categories of Realtors to whom I address this book, the more experienced Realtors (see Introduction).

I moved into the Denver area under quite humble circumstances. With a little over $500 to our name, and knowing but five people, my wife and I knew we would have to get established quickly in real estate and get up and running as quickly as possible. The following are the steps that I took:

1. **I studied the contracts** and other forms inside and out, since they were the vehicles to get me to the closing table.

2. **I decided to "learn the territory,"** i.e., learn the different residential subdivisions and the characteristics of the homes in those subdivisions. I set up a brochure file for each of the subdivisions, drove through them, previewed homes there, and

in general tried to become as knowledgeable as I could about homes in those subdivisions.

3. Whenever a real estate-related chamber of commerce or city council meeting was held, I would attend and meet as many people as I could to maximize my **networking capabilities**. This also helped me become more familiar with the different cities and municipalities in my immediate area and their economies and problems.

4. **I would buy breakfast or lunch for other successful Realtors** in my company and other companies and ask questions of them, trying to get my learning curve up to speed as quickly as possible. Everybody was quite helpful and provided me with a lot of information. I would then copy appropriate methods of operation and ideas from these individuals and assimilate them into my own program. I found that the key was to copy from only the very best!

5. **I picked a geographic farm** and started knocking on doors to see the people, learn the lingo, and build my sphere of influence.

6. **I took as much floor time as I could get.** Many times the busier, more productive salespeople were happy to have me take their floor time and it helped me to pick up buyers and sellers. Realtors may not be wildly enthusiastic about floor time, thinking it is somewhat old-fashioned and not relevant, but the office phone does ring with buyers and sellers looking for help, and using the techniques found in HOW TO CONVERT A PHONE CALL INTO A SALE discussed in

Chapter 3, pages 87-89, one can sharpen one's skills in this area.

7. **The Buddy System.** It helped me tremendously to have another agent work with me on my very first buyer. We told the buyer that she was my first; she was very nice and I was able to watch my colleague and fellow Realtor as he qualified that buyer, showed homes to her, wrote the contract, placed the loan, and went to the closing. I tagged along for all of these activities. The key here was I learned what happened in sequence to work with a buyer from start to finish, and it was much easier to learn and remember for that reason. I did not realize it at the time, but this was on-the-job training, and it was so very helpful for me.

8. **I asked questions of everybody all the time** as I was trying to assimilate as much knowledge and information in as short a time as possible.

9. **I specialized in a geographic farm area** early on in my career. Initially, I lacked confidence because I was so unfamiliar with different subdivisions. However, I moved into a newer subdivision and began prospecting and farming, and my confidence increased as I got more and more business from my farming activities in that subdivision.

10. **Checklists were developed** to help me become better organized. I arranged my time carefully and placed a dollar value on it (See the Dollar-Productive Activity sheet shown in the Appendix).

11. **Appearance is very important.** I made it a point to dress neatly and with fashionable clothes, remembering that "one does not have a second chance to make a first impression." To this day

and every working day I still wear my sport coat or suit and quite often a tie.

I developed an attitude of giving of myself and being "other directed." I tried to find people who had home-related problems and then took action to help them solve those problems. I tried always to do a little more than was required, and of course to work in an ethical manner.

Making Sure My Attitude and Motivation Are Positive

Throughout my sales career and even before going into sales as I was growing up, I have been intrigued about why certain people have a good attitude and are motivated to succeed while others do not. They appear to have everything going for them, e.g., good looks, a pleasing personality, good sales and closing instincts, and the like, but they just do not seem to get very far in the sales world. Then I would see another person whose demeanor was rather abrupt and yet did quite well.

So, I started doing research into why some people succeed in sales and others do not. Of course, as mentioned earlier in this chapter, we obviously need to have goals, but what else do we need?

I once again refer back to Earl Nightingale in his best-selling recording, *The Strangest Secret*. I referenced him earlier, but his message is so compelling and his points so well taken that in my opinion he bears quoting here again as well. As he says, the key to success, and the key to failure, is that we become what we think about.

Nightingale quotes Marcus Aurelius, the great Roman Emperor who said, "A man's life is what his thoughts make of it." If we think in positive terms, we will get positive results, and if we think in negative terms, we will get negative results.

It is logical then to ask why we don't think in positive terms more often, and at least in part, the answer is that many of us take our mind for granted because it is given to us at birth and is free. And we must control our thinking because our mind is neutral and will absorb whatever we put into it. To put positive thoughts into our mind is a challenge because during the first 18 years of our lives, if we grew up in fairly average, reasonably positive homes, experts say we were told "no!" or what we could not do, more than 148,000 times. The question is how often do we suppose we were told what we could accomplish in life? If the truth be known, many people cannot remember being told what they could accomplish more than three or four times in that entire period of time. Whatever the number, for most of us, the "yes!" responses we received simply in any way, shape or form did not balance out the "no!" responses. Leading behavioral researchers have told us that as much as 77 percent of everything we think about is negative, counterproductive, and works against us.

So for the vast majority of us, our minds are at a decided disadvantage, as so much of the input into our minds is negative. The human brain will do anything possible if we tell it to do it often enough and strongly enough!

The question then becomes how we place positive input into our minds. First, we need to get back to basics and realize that the quality of our life starts with the choices we make. Along this line, I highly recommend the best-selling book by Darren Hardy called *The Compound Effect*. As Darren says, success comes as a result of the operating system called the compound effect. What we really need is a new plan of action to create new behaviors and habits. The compound effect is "the principle of reaping huge rewards from a series of small, smart choices" (page 9).

Darren says that from the time we are born, "the life we end up with is simply an accumulation of all the choices we make" (page 23). Every choice starts as behavior that over time becomes a habit. Decisions shape our destiny. He says we are responsible for what we do, don't do, and how we respond to what is done to us. Regardless of the outcome of the election, or how bad the economy is, we are still in 100 percent control of ourselves.

As the great philosopher Jim Rohn said, "The day you graduate from childhood to adulthood is the day you take full responsibility for your life."

So the choices we make result in habits, and the goal for all of us is to establish in our lives the highest number of good, effective habits, and strive to minimize or eliminate the most bad, or ineffective habits. Aristotle said many years ago that "we are what we repeatedly do." The great achievers in life all share one common trait – they all have good habits! As Hardy emphasizes, a compound effect exists here: one good habit can result in a disproportionally large number of additional good habits, and the same is true in reverse for bad habits.

To summarize Hardy's formula for a maximally successful life, it is as follows:

YOU → CHOICE (decision) + BEHAVIOR (action) + HABIT (repeated action) + COMPOUNDED (time) = GOALS.

A great book was published recently titled *The Power of Habit*, by Charles Duhigg. In his book he emphasizes the power of habitual routines. He says, "Once you see everything as a bunch of habits, it's like someone gave you a flashlight and a crowbar and you can get to work." The noted author, John C. Maxwell, expands upon this statement with the following: "You will never change your life until you change something you do daily." The secret of success is found in your daily routines.

To learn how to establish these daily routines so they become habits as quickly and effectively as possible, I highly recommend the formative, ground-breaking research provided by B.J. Fogg, Ph.D., in his book, *Tiny Habits*. B.J. says to take the behavior you wish to become a part of you and make it "tiny" and very attainable. For example, if you want to develop the habit of walking three miles each day, do not start by trying to walk that far right away or you will get discouraged and quit before you even start. Rather, start "tiny" by doing something each day that is easy to do but related to walking, like just putting on your walking shoes each day. This becomes your "tiny behavior" and is your only act that you need to accomplish at the start of your new habit formation process. You tell yourself "I don't have to walk today, I just need to make sure I put on my walking shoes each day."

Then it will become easier to go out with your walking shoes on and initially walk just a few blocks. B.J. says the key is to start "tiny" but to do the same routine each day and at approximately the same time. You keep the bar low so as your motivation fluctuates day to day, you minimize the risk of getting discouraged and giving up on the possibility of walking at all. As you achieve interim goals, e.g., walking even those initial first few blocks, B.J. says it is important to celebrate that success and subsequent successes as you reach milestones, e.g., the first mile, then one and one-half miles, and on toward the three-mile goal. The points made in B.J.'s book are very helpful for any of us that have difficulty setting up behavior routines that eventually become habits.

Jim Rohn says, "Life is simply a collection of experiences; our goal should be to increase the frequency and the intensity of the good experiences. Positive habits and behaviors applied consistently will be the hallmark of winning against virtually any competition."

Harvey Mackay is a Minnesota-based businessman and author. I have read his books and articles for years. In one of his great essays entitled "Attitude is Everything," he spoke about a close friend of his named Jerry who was a manager of a restaurant. He asked Jerry how he could be such a positive person all the time. Jerry replied, "Each morning I wake up and say to myself, 'Jerry, you have two choices today: You can choose to be in a good mood, or you can choose to be in a bad mood.' I choose to be in a good mood. Each time something bad happens, I can choose to be a victim, or I can choose to learn from it.

Every time someone comes to me complaining, I can choose to accept their complaining, or I can point out the positive side of life. I choose the positive side of life."

Mackay continues by saying, "Life is all about choices. When you cut away all the junk, every situation is a choice. You choose how you react to situations. You choose how people will affect your mood. You choose to be in a good mood or a bad mood. The bottom line: It's your choice how you live life."

One of the most compelling and accurate descriptions of "Attitude" has been given by Chuck Swindoll, a religious educator, and I would like to share it with you here:

Attitude

The longer I live, the more I realize the impact of attitude on life. It is more important than the past, than education, than money, than circumstances, than failures, than successes, than what other people think or say or do. It is more important than appearance, giftedness, or skill. It will make or break a company, a church, a home. The remarkable thing is we have a choice every day regarding the attitude we will embrace for that day. We cannot change our past … we cannot change the fact that people will act in a certain way. We cannot change the inevitable. The only thing we can do is play on the one string we have, and that is our attitude. I am convinced that life is 10 percent what happens to me and 90 percent how I react to it. And so it is with you. We are in charge of our Attitude.

So much more can be said about attitude and motivation, and over the course of my 50+ years in real estate I have collected articles, quotes, and sayings that best capture the essence of those traits. One person told me that the individual that is the epitome of success approaches each day with the "have to" attitude rather than the "I would like to" attitude. In other words, the "have to" person drills down and focuses on getting the daily activities done; it is not an option with him or her. If the "like to" attitude exists, the feeling is, "Oh well, if it does not get done today, no big deal. It will happen tomorrow." If a lot of these "like to thoughts" accumulate, one's success pattern falls by the wayside and we get into the mental condition of "drift." This condition is all too common and will lead to ineffectiveness, inefficiency, and a wandering mind. Continued focus on the objective is critical!

An attitude of always doing the very best you can is stated very well in Charles Schwab's Ten Commandments of Success.

1. *Work Hard*

Hard work is the best investment a man can make.

2. *Study Hard*

Knowledge enables a man to work more intelligently and effectively.

3. *Have Initiative*

Ruts often deepen into graves.

4. *Love Your Work*

Then you will find pleasure in mastering it.

5.   *Be Exact*

Slipshod methods bring slipshod results.

6.   *Have the Spirit of Conquest*

Thus, you can successfully battle and overcome difficulties.

7.   *Cultivate Personality*

Personality is to a man what perfume is to the flower.

8.   *Help and Share with Others*

The real test of business greatness lies in giving opportunity to others.

9.   *Be Democratic*

Unless you feel right toward your fellow men, you can never be a successful leader of men.

10.   *In All Things Do Your Best*

The man who has done his best has done everything.

The man who has done less than his best has done nothing.

In Schwab's 10 commandments he mentions quite a few other traits of the person whose positive attitude will always put him in good stead in life and in business.

Number 5, "Be Exact," is one that has always been import-ant to me. I am constantly amazed by the lack of detail that is found throughout my day. For example, I always proofread my e-mails before pushing the "send" button. I believe the hallmark of a real professional in any field of endeavor is shown by the well-written, correctly-spelled e-mail or letter.

Especially in our business of real estate, attention to detail is critical. Within the last several years, as detailed as my real estate team and I have been, we neglected to write into the contract in representing the buyer, the inclusion of a $10,000 hot tub that was in the backyard of the home. In the final outcome, our lack of writing in that the hot tub/spa was included in the sale resulted in our having to "buy" a replacement hot tub for the buyer, costing me and my real estate team approximately $10,000! You can bet that this mistake will never happen again!

In my opinion, we should always have an attitude of striving to do the very best we can. An article that I read approximately 25 years ago stayed with me and made a big impression on me. I always thought that certainly 99.9 percent in any field of endeavor was more than good enough – until I read that article.

Strive for Perfection or Else

Written by Gary Sheer

If 99.9 percent is good enough, then

- ▶ Two million documents will be lost by the IRS this year.
- ▶ 811,000 faulty rolls of 35 mm. film will be loaded this year.
- ▶ 22,000 checks will be deducted from the wrong bank accounts this year.

- ▶ 1,314 phone calls will be misplaced by telecommunication services every minute.

- ▶ 12 babies will be given to the wrong parents each day.

- ▶ 268,500 defective tires will be shipped this year.

- ▶ 14,208 defective personal computers will be shipped this year.

- ▶ 103,260 income tax returns will be processed incorrectly this year.

- ▶ 2,488,200 books will be shipped in the next 12 months with the wrong cover.

- ▶ 5,517,200 cases of soft drinks produced in the next 12 months will be flatter than a bad tire.

- ▶ Every day, two plane landings at O'Hare International Airport in Chicago will be unsafe.

- ▶ 3,056 copies of tomorrow's Wall Street Journal will be missing one of the three sections.

- ▶ 18,322 pieces of mail will be mishandled in the next hour.

- ▶ 291 pacemaker operations will be performed incorrectly this year.

- ▶ 880,000 credit cards in circulation will turn out to have incorrect cardholder information on their magnetic strips.

- ▶ $9,690 will be spent today, tomorrow, next Thursday, and every day in the future on defective, often unsafe, sporting equipment.

- ▶ 55 malfunctioning automatic teller machines will be installed in the next 12 months.

- ▶ 20,000 incorrect drug prescriptions will be written in the next 12 months.

- ▶ 114,500 mismatched pairs of shoes will be shipped this year.

> ▶ $761,900 will be spent in the next 12 months on tapes and compact discs that won't play.
>
> ▶ 107 incorrect medical procedures will be performed by the end of the day today.
>
> ▶ 315 entries in Webster's Third New International Dictionary of the English Language will turn out to be misspelled.

I received the above article from my good friend, Bob Wolff, who is a very successful Realtor in Laguna Niguel, California. It was written quite a few years ago, so the figures today will probably be even higher and more alarming.

Bob suggests that we calculate our losses attributable to a "good enough" attitude and redouble our efforts towards achieving zero defects. He, in my opinion, is the poster child for living life with a positive attitude. As he says, "The single most important source of business is attitude and striving to do the very best that we can in all situations."

I personally believe we should always strive for perfection, but never forget that true, ultimate perfection is not totally possible in this life.

However, it is the "striving" for that perfection that counts. In this regard, I refer frequently to my "garbage can" story. Our greatest danger in performing our daily activities is letting other people dump negative "garbage" on us. Unfortunately, we always have those in our lives who want to dump their problems (garbage) on us.

So, my story starts by saying that it is a cold, January evening in my home state of Wisconsin. My wife and I have scrimped and saved, and our brand-new carpet was just installed today. It is evening and she and I are sitting with our shoes off in front of the crackling fireplace in our family room; we can smell the aroma of the burning wood and the new carpet, and our toes are squiggling in that carpet and we are totally relaxed.

At this moment, the doorbell rings. We go to the door, and a garbage man is standing there in bib overalls with the filthiest can of garbage you have ever seen. He pushes us aside, hurriedly steps in and starts dumping this filthy garbage all over our brand-new carpet! The question is: "what would we do?" Why for sure and at the very least we would ask him to leave immediately and shove him out the door with his garbage can as quickly as we can.

The point is: while none of us would allow anyone to come in and dump physical garbage on our carpet, whether brand new carpet or not, how many of us on a daily basis allow people to dump mental garbage in our minds?

I never forgot this story and whenever I feel I am being dumped upon, the first thing I do is to recognize that this is in fact happening, and then secondly, I pull down a mental shield so that the garbage does not hit and infect me.

We need to keep that shield "at the ready" as we go through our day so that we can keep "garbage dumpers" from penetrating our psyche.

A good description of an individual who is a winner in the fight against garbage dumping and negativism is found in the following:

Winner vs Loser

by: Author Unknown, Source Unknown

The Winner is always part of the answer;
The Loser is always part of the problem.

The Winner always has a plan;
The Loser always has an excuse.

The Winner says, "Let me do it for you;"
The Loser says, "That is not my job."

The Winner sees an answer for every problem;
The Loser sees a problem for every answer.

The Winner says," It may be difficult, but it is possible;"
The Loser says, "It may be possible, but it is too difficult."

When a Winner makes a mistake, he says," I was wrong;"
When a Loser makes a mistake, he says, "It wasn't my fault."

A Winner makes commitments;
A Loser makes promises.

Winners have dreams;
Losers have schemes.

Winners say, "I must do something;"
Losers say, "Something must be done."

Winners are a part of the team;
Losers are apart from the team.

No one is saying that being in the "winner" category in each of the above is easy, but again, it is the consistent striving – not giving up, each day – that makes the difference.

In fact, on our journey toward perfecting our understanding of attitude and motivation as they impact our daily lives, we should expect some speed bumps along the way. Harvey Mackay, quoted previously, stresses that mistakes are among life's great teachers. As he says, "There are really no mistakes in life, there are only lessons. Try as we may, we will eventually mess up, but how we respond to our errors determines how smart we really are." As Eleanor Roosevelt said, "Learn from the mistakes of others. You can't live long enough to make them all yourself."

The great motivational speaker, Brian Tracy, states that "Failure is just feedback," and Winston Churchill emphasizes that "Success consists of going from failure to failure without loss of enthusiasm."

J.K. Rowling, author of the best-selling *Harry Potter* book series, delivered her commencement address at the annual meeting of the Harvard Alumni Association on June 8, 2008. In that address she spoke of the benefits of failure. She says, "Some failure in life is inevitable; it is impossible to live without failing at something unless you live so cautiously that you might as well not have lived at all, in which case you fail by default."

For her, failure meant a stripping away of the unessential. Further, she says, "The knowledge that you have emerged wiser and stronger from setbacks means that you are ever after secure in your ability to survive. You will never truly know yourself, or the strength of your relationships, until both have been tested by adversity. Such knowledge is a true gift, for all that it is painfully won, and it has been worth more to me than any qualification I ever earned." She adds, "Happiness lies in knowing that life is not a check list of acquisition or achievements."

The late, great head coach of the Dallas Cowboys, Tom Landry, spoke of the struggles for success related to coaching his players as follows: "You show them what they don't want to see. You tell them what they don't want to hear. You make them do what they don't want to do so they can become the person they always wanted to be."

As mentioned earlier, many of us do find speed bumps along the road, and I have found the following to be helpful as I encounter those bumps:

> *I asked for strength*
> *and I was given difficulties*
> *to make me strong.*
>
> *I asked for wisdom*
> *and was given problems*
> *to solve.*
>
> *I asked for prosperity*
> *and was given energy*
> *to work.*
>
> *I asked for courage*
> *and was given obstacles*

to overcome.

I asked for love and was given people to help.
I asked for favors and was given opportunities.
I received nothing I wanted, but everything
I needed.

On a lighter note, and when speaking of the ultimate in two different approaches to attitude, I saved the following from an old clipping:

Many years ago, a large American shoe manufacturer sent two sales reps out to different parts of the Australian outback to see if they could drum up some business among the aborigines. Sometime later, the company received telegrams from both agents. The first one said, "No business here, natives don't wear shoes." The second one said, "Great opportunity here, natives don't wear shoes!"

This is a very concrete example of "the glass is half-full, not half-empty" approach, and is similar to the "Acres of Diamonds" book by Russell Conwell. In this classic parable, Conwell speaks to the fact that we often dream of fortunes to be made elsewhere, when we should be open to the possibility that the "acres of diamonds" are all around us.

In my opinion, the following is about as succinct a summary of attitude and success as any I have found. The author is unknown:

If you think you are beaten, you are,
If you think you dare not, you don't.

If you like to win, but you think you can't,
It is almost certain you won't.

If you think you'll lose, you're lost
For out of the world we find,
Success begins with a fellow's will—
It's all in the state of mind.

If you think you are outclassed, you are,
You've got to think high to rise,
You've got to be sure of yourself before
You can ever win a prize.

Life's battles don't always go
To the stronger or faster man,
But soon or late the man who wins
Is the man WHO THINKS HE CAN!

Years ago, as I was searching for meaning in my life, I read a poem that I have never forgotten; it spoke to me about what it really meant for an individual to be a success. It was listed in a newspaper column by syndicated columnist Abigail Van Buren:

Success

You can use most any measure when you're speaking of success.

You can measure it in fancy home, expensive car, or dress.

But the measure of your real success is the one you cannot spend.

It's the way your kids describe you when they're talking to a friend.

– Christy H. Richards, Fielding, Utah

Our kids know us better than anyone does! Listen to them carefully and sincerely praise them such that they will talk favorably about you when talking to others!

Finally, I love the statement from an anonymous, apparently fun-loving person who sums up his life with the best and most fulfilling statement about how to live life to the fullest:

Life

Is not a journey to the grave
With the intention of arriving safely
In a pretty and well-preserved body,
but rather to skip in broadside,
thoroughly used up, totally worn out,
and loudly proclaiming,
"WOW! WHAT A RIDE!!!"

Founding and Then Selling My Own Real Estate Company

When I started selling residential real estate over fifty years ago, the furthest thing in my mind was setting up my own real estate company. Like most Realtors starting out, I aligned myself with a reputable real estate firm for the training it would provide me and for the reputation it had.

However, as the years progressed and as I became more successful, I got to thinking about the fact that I was working really hard and the firm I was working with had no pension and/or 401K program. It occurred to me that while I was earning good money, I needed to set aside some dollars for the time when I would no longer be selling because I might have developed a disability that would not allow me to show homes. Several of my colleagues with the same firm shared with me that they were experiencing the same concerns. We went to our employing company's personnel department and asked if they would consider setting up such a program; they gave us an unfavorable response.

So I suggested to four of my colleagues that we meet and discuss our options. This was in early 1981. We decided to contact a very sharp real estate attorney and we paid him to tell us our options; he suggested that he could set up a "defined benefit" and a "money purchase IRS-approved plan" for each of us. He explained the advantages of those plans, and it became obvious to us that this was the way for us to go. He told us that in many instances we could funnel pre-tax dollars into those programs, and that would enable us to have a plan in place to legally set aside dollars for our retirement.

I do not recall the dollar amounts necessary to establish the plans, but those dollars and the fees payable to the attorney paled in comparison to the savings that we realized over the ensuing years. We learned that the maximum benefits to be derived from the plans would be realized only if we set up our own real estate company. All of us were very successful in our own right, and the strong temptation was to just continue with the status quo and stay with our current company. However, we all felt that we would always kick ourselves if we knew about this tremendous opportunity and did not at least give it a good hard try.

At the same time, the concern that occurred to us was that our clients might not list and sell with us if we were on our own as opposed to selling for our current strong, reputable established firm. We really did not know the answer to this question, but we worried about our clients saying something to the effect of, "We love you Jim, but we are concerned about dealing with a brand new firm." We lost several clients that elected not to go with us because of this kind of reasoning.

All this notwithstanding, we decided to give it a go and handed in our resignations!

I will never forget my March, 1981 breakfast meeting with my mentor and the sales manager of my firm. I was up most of the night before our breakfast meeting, trying to rehearse what I was going to say and how I would say it as I told him I was resigning. I loved my mentor like a brother, and it was a very, very difficult meeting. I managed to get through it and, of course, he was giving me all the reasons why I should stay and not move on.

(Parenthetically, my big consolation in all this was that this same mentor/manager resigned from the firm approximately six months later!)

As I look back, we were fortunate in that each of the five new partners in our newly-formed company, The Kentwood Company, had characteristics and attributes that coalesced and complemented each other, making for a good partnership. All of us had been listing and selling homes and would continue to do so. However, each of us in retrospect had traits and talents that would contribute to the success of our fledging company. Two of our partners had managerial experience and knew how to run a successful company. One of the partners had a distinct ability to list entire new home subdivisions. He knew how to set up and successfully run new, on-site home sales centers. This ability resulted in listings for our company from buyer prospects that would need to sell their homes to buy the new homes that my partner was offering; the result was an immediate influx of new listings and subsequent sales. And of course, even though I had an MBA in marketing, my greatest talent was a decided ability to sell homes and get listings, so I was able to bring in sufficient listings and sales during the early years to work in the trenches, so to speak, as I helped keep the company afloat and the doors open.

The commission-sharing plan that we established was quite simple, but it worked! We had five partners, and the partner that brought in the listing or sale would get 80 percent of the total commission value, and the other four of us would get 5 percent apiece. This program worked well for us in the early years. Of course, we all shared in the expenses but this program at least got us off the ground.

All five of us knew each other quite well, we trusted each other, and we knew that each of us in our own right was competent. Steven Covey, in his best-selling book, *The Speed of Trust*, speaks to the importance of this trust factor in any business endeavor.

In my opinion, the two overriding, necessary attributes for success in a business are competence and trust. In our case, my partners and I each had both attributes, and of course our clients needed to know that we possessed those traits. If the client knows that you are competent but has doubts about your trustworthiness, success will not follow you; on the other hand, if the client totally trusts you but knows you are new in the business and not very knowledgeable, they could have some significant reservations about using you. In our case, fortunately all five of us had those two attributes in abundance.

I must say that a scary moment occurred when all of us had to sign the paperwork for the newly executed lease for our company. But when you are 30+ years younger you rather gulp and say, "Well, what is the worst that can happen?" and then rationalize and say, "The good news is that in the United States we have the freedom to fail." Anyway, we were off to the races with our new company. We set up the company in March, 1981, and the interest rates were hovering around 20 percent. Scary times! The high interest rates were a real challenge!

During that first-year, high-interest time, we dealt with some transferees through our one-person relocation department. In order to get the employee to transfer, the transferring company often paid an interest differential. For example, if the employee was transferring to Denver from Houston and had a current 8 percent mortgage there, the transferring company would pay a monthly interest differential to the employee in an amount equal to the dollar difference between the monthly principal and interest payment at 8 percent, and the principal and interest payment at the current interest rate of, say, 20 percent in Denver. We have it so good today interest-rate-wise, and when clients complain about the current rate going up from, say, 3.5 percent to 4.5 percent, I tell them this background story, their eyes get big as saucers, and they complain no longer about "high" interest rates.

In our very early years we were fortunate to obtain the services of a really good Chief Financial Officer (CFO). He was with us for many years and was an invaluable asset to our company. Having a good financial person on board is crucial to a company's success, especially in the start-up years.

I distinctly remember our first holiday party at my home in December, 1981. Our entire company at that time consisted of the five partners, our spouses, and the secretary/administrative assistant and her husband. So that was our entire company, just 12 people! We had no additional salespeople (guess they were hedging their bets on whether or not we would make it). Now fast-forward to the year 2020. Kentwood closed sales volume in 2020 of $2,180,688 with 209 agents working out of four offices!
Billion

From the time we set up our firm we established a dress code of suit or sport coat for the guys and dress and/or pants for the ladies. We have relaxed this policy a bit for the guys allowing "smart casual" (no ties). However, the basic premise is if you dress for success you will feel better about yourself and will do a better job of selling yourself and your listing to your client. We have established a brand for Kentwood in which we believe we are one of the very few real estate firms in the Denver area where successful Realtors from other firms feel they can move up to, and where it really is a move up and not a lateral move.

As Kentwood Real Estate continued to grow and prosper, national real estate firms had come asking if we would be interested in selling our firm. Of course, we looked into opportunities as they presented themselves. We weren't sure we were really interested in selling, especially if the potential acquiring company was requiring us to change the name of our company. After several firms contacted us to no avail, we gave no further thought to a sale.

In 2007, two local Denver real estate individuals with previous connections to Kentwood offered to buy our company. They assured us that they were not interested in changing our name and would in fact keep the name and logo "as-is," a real plus from our point of view. This got our attention, and from the initiation of their interest in January 2007, to closing on May 18, 2007, the time frame was only about four months and our company was sold!

Each of the four owners, myself included, stayed on in a sales capacity and the company continued to do well. The two people to whom we sold the company subsequently sold to HomeServices of America, a Berkshire Hathaway affiliate, in 2016. That firm has approximately 43,258 agents working in 883 offices in 30 states and the District of Columbia. In 2020 the firm closed 346,161 transactions for a total sales volume of $152.2 Billion.

In summary, the five of us (four when we actually sold) were fortunate to assemble people with whom we had mutual trust and respect. We knew each of us was competent and trustworthy, and we brought on a very detailed and experienced CFO very early on. We just went for it and did not look back. We never gave a moment's thought to hiring a consulting firm to see if we were doing the right thing. It is so gratifying to drive through the metropolitan area of Denver and see our signs everywhere. The good Lord has shed his blessings upon us, has been good to us, was with us as we set up our company, and then has helped us as our company has grown over the last 40 years!

3.

How I Prospect
and Farm for Clients

Prospecting and People/Geographic
Farming

WHEN I FIRST started selling homes I was very nervous and uptight. I had sold pots and pans to get through college and, as mentioned earlier, I sold tickets to sales motivational congresses in New York City and in Colorado Springs and Pueblo, Colorado. But now my wife and I were in a strange town, Denver, where we knew very few people, and I was selling real estate on straight commission. I was determined to do everything I could so as not to fail. I spoke to one of my chief mentors, Sven Nylund, and asked him to please tell me what I needed to do to be assured that I would not fail or on the opposite side of the coin, what I had to do to be successful. I will never forget what he told me over 50 years ago. He said, "Jim, just three words – SEE THE PEOPLE!"

So, I began to figure out a plan and strategy for accomplishing that goal. Obviously I started selling homes many years ago, and you might think that some of the techniques and strategies that I will share with you in the following paragraphs are outdated and irrelevant or, at the very least, not as effective as they were when I began using them. I do realize that we have much more sophisticated computer programs and software today than we had back then, and e-mails and text messaging were not even born yet! However, I firmly believe that the ways to "see the people" that I am going to share with you here are just as effective, if not more effective, now than they were back then. So, join me as I cover these time-tested ways to prospect, see the people and get the sales.

Prospecting is the lifeblood of the real estate industry, and the root origin of the word "prospecting" as it relates to real estate in its essence refers to "looking out" at the world around us to see whom we might assist in finding a home they can afford, and a home that will make their life happier than it was the day before. To accomplish this goal, I realized that I needed to establish a purpose and an orderly process to my "looking out."

It was always evident to me that sales was a lucrative field. However, I wondered if I was getting my fair share. Sven told me eighty percent of the real estate sales are made by 20 percent of the people, and with his help I began to analyze what attributes the most successful real estate salespeople possessed in order for them to do so well. (1) They establish goals for themselves; (2) They are disciplined to work a program consistently; (3) They expect and welcome rejection as they strive toward achieving their goals; and (4) They are constantly trying to learn new techniques and ideas from the best people in their field, either through classes and seminars or through personal visits with the most successful real estate practitioners.

GOALS: As mentioned in the first part of Chapter 2, goal-setting is critically important for success in selling real estate. With this in mind, I established goals of meeting a certain number of prospects each month – some in person, some by telephone, some by letter, and some through a combination of these contact vehicles. Again, with my mentor Sven's help, I tried to determine how I would find these people, where were they? The following is what I learned about the best methods and techniques for reaching these prospects.

Sources of Prospects:

1. It became evident to me that **everyone was a prospect!** Almost every person I came in contact with during the day was a potential client or knew of a potential client. I found that this was at the same time the most frustrating and yet the most exciting aspect of my real estate profession. There was and is no limit to who can purchase, or when he or she can buy. That truly represented the opportunity of a lifetime for me unfolding itself anew each day!

    In this same light, I always enthusiastically told my story to as many people as possible. Along this line I developed a list of "Who I Know" (see attached at the end of this chapter) that helped me determine who I should be contacting as prospects. This is a great list and I still refer to it even today. I told the people who I was, what I was doing, that I loved real estate, and that if I was ever given the opportunity and honor to help them, I would give them the red carpet treatment and my full 100 percent effort. I handed out my card to everyone with whom I came in contact, like the shopkeeper, the bank teller and the bridge partner, asking each of them for their business. As I mentioned in a previous chapter, I was told that the biblical basis for prospecting is "ask and you shall receive," "seek and you shall find," "knock and it will be opened unto you." In other words, even the bible sanctions prospecting!

2. I also determined that the **reputation of my company** and its associates was another good source of business.

3. I **became active** in the local Chamber of Commerce and got to know effective commercial Realtors and leasing agents. I found out that they often knew about corporate moves before anyone else did and could be very helpful. I further determined that another source of business was my own company referral department. Prospects were comfortable dealing with me because they knew that I had a solid company behind me.

4. **Spheres of Influence**: My wife and I became involved in such activities and hobbies as carpooling, bowling, tennis, wine tasting, book clubs, traveling, homeowner's association, study groups, church, and the like. Each year I attended the National Association of Realtors (NAR) Convention as well as the Colorado Association of Realtors (CAR) Convention, and through meeting and developing relationships with other firms and Realtors around

the country, a considerable number of referrals back and forth resulted.

5. **National, state, and local referrals**: I always made sure that I paid a fair referral fee and that I reported back on each lead, thanking the referral company or the individual Realtors for their referrals.

6. **Print Advertising**: I advertised my active listings but found that I did not often sell the home that I was advertising off the ad for that home. However, I learned that the function of an ad is to get the phone to ring or get a response to the digital ad, not to necessarily sell the home on which the call was made. The prospect has several ads in front of him and he knows that if, for example, he needs a four-bedroom home and you tell him that the home he inquired about is a three-bedroom, he will move on. As soon as I told him it was a three-bedroom, he eliminated the home and quickly hung up. I found out right away that it was so important to have.... (see number 7 directly below)

7. **Effective telephone technique**: The following are some points that I found to be helpful: voice and courtesy are most important – they can't see your gestures. Answer Promptly; picture the person, and imagine you are right there with them, in person; smile when you speak; listen; don't bang the receiver down; THE MOST IMPORTANT POINT IS TO ASK QUESTIONS; HE WHO ASKS QUESTIONS IS IN CONTROL. Be selective — you'll lose the good ones because you've got appointments with unqualified buyers.

(See the attached "How to Convert a Phone Call into a Sale" at the end of this chapter for the complete listing of the techniques that I used and still use to this day). By the way, to motivate me to really treat each phone call seriously, I have a sign on my desk with $11,300 written on it, to remind me that each of my closings is equal to at least that amount of commission. This helps emphasize to me that each phone call could result in that amount of commission or more at closing, and therefore to treat that phone call with the utmost seriousness and respect.

Through all this it was becoming very evident to me that it was critical for me to place a dollar value on my time (see Appendix, Dollar-Productive Activities chart). I needed to be prepared by knowing my listing inventory, by regularly going on tour (our company still tours our new listings) and by consistently visiting the new home subdivisions. This information gave me a competitive edge in my knowledge of new models, innovative financing techniques, and the like.

8. **Geographic Farming**: Although considered primarily as a listing tool, farming is also an excellent source of buyers. You will be talking with someone about listing their home, and they will mention that they have a friend who is coming into town. Any activity that places you in eye-to-eye contact with prospects is most important. Unfortunately, the average salesman spends relatively few hours per month in this activity.

After about nine months in the business my wife and I purchased our first home in a newer tract area called The Dam West subdivision in Aurora, Colorado. My goal was to dominate the listings in this area. I started by setting up a three-ring book binder, categorizing each of the homes in the area within that binder by their model names. Soon I had a complete list of everything that sold and that was on the market, by model, and I was becoming the expert in the area. Other brokers in the office were asking for my opinion of value on specific homes in the subdivision, and appraisers were calling me for similar opinions and to get comparable sales. My wife would help me drive the area each day looking for "For Sale by Owner" signs. Each time I obtained a new listing, I would personally walk to each of the 15 homes surrounding the listed property, knocking on their doors and telling those 15 owners that I had just listed the property down the street, and asking them if they knew of anyone who would make a nice neighbor for them; or if they themself might be interested in selling. It was almost without fail that one of those 15 homes would go on the market shortly after my listing went on the market; so, this was a great source of listing leads. Additionally, every holiday season I would hand-deliver to each homeowner a calendar for the upcoming year.

In a span of a year or two I reached my goal of controlling seventy percent of the listings in the subdivision! Later when I moved out of the subdivision into a higher-priced subdivision where my wife and I currently live, I used similar marketing techniques. However, I supplemented my other techniques by compiling and producing a directory for the owners in that new subdivision. I am also fortunate enough to have participated in over 120 home sales in the subdivision!

9. **Open Houses**: I found that I very seldom ended up selling the listing that I was holding open, but I also found that the open house was an excellent source of buyers. How did I get their name, address, and phone numbers? I had a sign-in registration yellow pad (nothing fancy) on the kitchen counter and on top I wrote in the date, name, address, and phone number headings, as well as the address of the home being held open. As the people came through, I asked them if they would sign in so that later I could show the owner that I had not been sitting around doing nothing, i.e., that people had been coming through. I would number lines on the yellow sheet from 1 to 10 and then I would sign in a friend's name, address, and phone number for number 1. Sure enough, all succeeding people filled it out with exactly the same pieces of information, including the all-important phone number. It still works to this day and I always get the phone number and address by using this "pieces-of-information" method.

10. **Newspaper Clippings**: Whenever I saw a press release on anyone that I knew, especially past clients, I would clip it out and send it to the individual along with a hand-written congratulatory note. It is surprising how few people will take the time to do this, but people do remember, and I found this to be an excellent method of prospecting.

11. **Corporate Contacts**:

A. I worked hard to develop key contacts in the personnel and operational end of the business. One of the best methods I found was to have breakfast or lunch with the individuals in those areas of the company. I learned to take my time and not come across as being too forceful, quick, or anxious.

B. I found that it was important to give of myself and develop the attitude of not being overly concerned about what I would receive in return. I knew that if I cast my bread on the waters, so to speak that it would come back to me in even bigger amounts.

I would offer to spend a day with a man and his wife who were contemplating a move but weren't absolutely sure yet. I found that the potential transferee and his or her boss would be impressed that I was taking time out to help them without any promise of immediate business in return. The boss would feel guilty, especially if the potential transferee did not accept the job or if a job was not offered, and consequently I found that he would do his best to get me more business. I would offer to keep the corporation up to date on market conditions, interest rate fluctuations, and the like --- no strings attached. I found that I did not need to give gifts or "payoffs" each time I got a referral, and that giving the best possible service was my best insurance policy for obtaining more clients.

C. I always reported back to the referral source with a status report and to give a sincere thank you!

12. **Satisfied Past Customers**: This is the best referral source of all!!!

A. I always tried to do a little bit more for my customer than did the next Realtor.

B. I set up a follow-up system.

C. Sven, my mentor, reminded me that our clients are constantly coming into contact with other people and other Realtors who can influence them to move away from me and work with one of them. Thus, the importance of a regular, consistent system of keeping in touch is all the more important.

D. I learned not to walk away from my customers' problems. I stayed with them until the problem was solved.

E. I did a good job, and then: I ALWAYS ASKED FOR REFERRALS!

F. I worked on developing a good understanding of human nature and tried to be able to "psych out" the client's physical and psychological needs and wants. I attempted to understand what was motivating the buyer. I understand and have learned that buyers must make five definite decisions: (a) They must decide that they have a NEED; (b) They must decide that the THING offered fills that need; (c) They must decide that the SOURCE from which they are buying is right; (d) They must decide the PRICE is right; (e) They must decide the TIME to buy is now.

After working with the above 12 sources of prospects, if you still could use some additional sources of business, take a look at the following list of "memory joggers." I referred to them earlier in this chapter, and they have been an invaluable source of prospects for me.

Who Do You Know?

- From your old job?
- From school or college?
- Because of your favorite sports or hobbies?
- From your church?
- From civic activities?
- Because you rent or own your own home?
- Because you lived in other neighborhoods?
- Who sold you your automobile?
- Who sells you gas, tires, or lubrication?
- Through your children?
- Through your wife or husband?
- From lodge or club?
- Who sells you meat?
- Who sells you groceries?
- Who sold you your refrigerator?
- Who is a nurse?

- Who is a lawyer?
- Who sold your spouse/significant other their clothes?
- Who runs your delicatessen?
- Who manages your local theater?
- Who tends to your pet(s) when they are sick?
- Who appraises real estate?
- Who made your awnings, storm windows?
- Who is your physician?
- Who is your dentist?
- Who is your druggist?
- Who heads your local Veteran's organization?
- Who is your son or daughter's scoutmaster?
- Who sells new and used cars?
- Who sells you shoes?
- Who sold you your pet?
- Who is your best luncheon club friend?
- Who is your painter and decorator?
- Who is your postmaster or letter carrier?
- Who owns the dairy where you buy milk, eggs, and butter?
- Who heads up local organizations like the Lions Club and the Kiwanis?
- Who manages or owns your local Home Depot, Ace Hardware or Best Buy store?

- Who is your local printer?
- Who plays bridge with your wife/husband/significant other?
- Who styles your wife's/husband's hair?
- Who sold you your fence?
- Who is the manager of your FedEx office?
- Who was best man/bridesmaid at your wedding?
- Who sold you your piano?
- Who gives your children music lessons?
- Who sold you your wedding ring?
- Who fixes your watch?
- Who sells you hats?
- Who sells you suits?
- Who owns the hotel nearest you?
- Who took and produced your latest family photos?
- Who edits your local newspaper?
- Who is on your election board?
- Who are your buddies in the American Legion?
- Who serves you lunch?
- Who heads the local parent-teacher's association?
- Who bought that house in your neighborhood?
- Who sold you your glasses?
- Who plays the organ at your church?

- Who prints your stationery?

- Who is the principal of your high school?

- Who services your furnace, central air conditioning systems and hot water heater?

- Who is the chief of your fire department?

- Who is your chief of police?

- Who heads your bank?

- Who owns your bowling alley?

- Who is your local mortgage loan officer?

- Who sells you office supplies?

- Who sold you your furniture?

- Who does your dry cleaning?

- Who is your florist?

- Who repairs your cable and television?

- Who sells you fishing tackle?

- Who is expecting a new baby?

- Who bought a new home?

- Who has a business that is booming because of current economic conditions?

- Who stores your rugs?

In summary, I found that by following the points referenced above, I could be, and was, very successful in obtaining a steady stream of potential clients. However, in the final analysis it is all about relationships. Clients need to know that we are competent and that they can trust us to do a good job as well as doing the right thing for them. If we do this, everything else falls into place and we will have as much business as we can handle.

How to Convert a Phone Call Into a Sale

1. Telephone Technique in General

a.   **Voice and courtesy** are paramount – they can't see your gestures.

b.   **Answer promptly** – If looking for the information on the home they are calling about, let them know you appreciate their patience… and thank them for waiting.

c.   **Identify yourself.**

d.   **Sit tall and stand tall** – Bad posture leads to a tense and strained voice.

e.   **Picture the person** – Imagine you are right there, in person, talking to the person.

f.   **Use lower tones** – High-pitched voices turn people off.

g.   **Smile when you speak.**

h.   **Speak slow and low** – Take time to save time – get in tune with them.

i.   **Be enthusiastic!**

j.   **Listen** – God gave us two ears and one mouth and there's a reason for it; we should listen twice as much as we speak.

k.   **Don't bang the receiver down** – Wait for the other person to hang up before you hang up.

2. Handling a Real Estate Telephone Inquiry

a. **What property are you inquiring about?** Ask questions to keep in control.

b. **Did you learn about it through an ad? Sign?**

c. **Do you prefer that style of house?** (let them talk.) Listen.

d. This particular home is priced at $449,500 (as an example). **Is this the price range you are looking in?**

e. **Are you renting or do you own a home?** Also determine, if possible, if they have ever bought a home before. This question also helps you ascertain if a listing possibility exists.

f. **How long have you been looking for a home?** (if, e.g., two years, probably should forget it!)

g. **Mr. Prospect, if I were to find you just the home you want – exactly what you are looking for – would you be willing to invest in that home today?** (if not, why not? Maybe they need the equity from their present home.)

h. Somewhere in the questioning sequence, possibly here, mention that the home-purchasing decision is a big one and should not be jumped into, so to speak. This statement throws the prospect off guard because he or she thinks you <u>want</u> them to jump into it. At this point, emphasize your function as **Counselor**; just like the doctor cannot accurately diagnose over the phone, neither can you, and you would hate for the prospect to make a big decision – buying (investing) in a home – without all the necessary facts at his or her disposal. Therefore:

i. **Has anyone ever explained to you how a lender in your city would qualify you for a loan?** Tell them you would like to do this, as well as have the opportunity to answer questions and give advice. In other words, giving them the facts they need to make an intelligent decision.

j. **Get the appointment** – Make sure **both** husband and wife or significant other or friend will come to meet with you; if they are truly interested in working with you, they will be happy to come to your office. Emphasize the ultimate TIME savings to the buyer prospect of having this initial meeting. Also, do not ask if they would like an appointment, but rather phrase the question as follows: "How about getting together for a brief appointment at 5 p.m. next Tuesday, or would 5:30 be better?"

k. **Send both an e-mail and a hand-written letter confirming the appointment.**

l. **Be selective** – You'll lose the "good" ones because you've got too many appointments with the "bad" ones. Sell the appointment, NOT the property. Make the client want to hear your story.   Value your time!

4.

How I Manage My Time and Energy

Time Management

S INCE I HAVE been in sales for most of my adult life, I have always been acutely aware of the importance of time.

I have mentioned the impact that my mentor, Sven Nylund, had on my sales career and on my life in general. Early in my sales career I copied a note from one of Sven's talks and have tried to live by its message for my entire career. He said that "Time is Money." He goes on to reference Ben Franklin, who once compared time to money. Franklin said that time is like money in that it is a capital asset, but he goes on to further state that, "unlike money and other assets <u>you cannot borrow time, you cannot hoard it, nor can you work exceptionally hard and earn</u>

more of it. All you can do is spend it, and how you spend it is the difference between success and failure."

Expanding on this, Alan Lakein in his classic book, *How to Get Control of Your Time and Your Life*, says we should care about our time because "Time is Life! It is irreversible and irreplaceable. To waste your time is to waste your life, but to master your time is to master your life and make the most of it." Along this same line of thought, one of my good friends and a past client as well sent me the following e-mail in December, 2002, and I was so impressed with it that I have retained it all these years and would like to share it with you here.

Imagine...

There is a bank that credits your account each morning with $86,400. It carries over no balance from day to day. Every evening it deletes whatever part of the balance you failed to use during the day. What Would you do? Draw out ALL OF IT, of Course!

Each of us has such a bank. Its name is TIME. Every morning, it credits you with 86,400 seconds. Every night it writes off, as lost, whatever of this you have failed to invest to good purpose. It carries over no balance. It allows no overdraft. Each day it opens a new account for you. Each night it burns the remains of the day. If you fail to use the day's deposits, the loss is yours. There is no going back. There is no drawing against the "tomorrow." You must live in the present on today's deposits. Invest it so as to get from it the utmost in health, happiness, and success!

The clock is running! Make the most of today.

To realize the value of ONE YEAR, ask a student who failed a grade.

To realize the value of ONE MONTH, ask a mother who gave birth to a premature baby.

To realize the value of ONE WEEK, ask the editor of a weekly newspaper.

To realize the value of ONE HOUR, ask the lovers who are waiting to meet.

To realize the value of ONE MINUTE, ask a person who missed the train.

To realize the value of ONE SECOND, ask the person who just avoided an accident.

To realize the value of ONE MILLISECOND, ask the person who won a silver medal in the Olympics.

Treasure every moment that you have! And treasure it more because you shared it with someone special, special enough to spend your time.

And remember that time waits for no one. Yesterday is history. Tomorrow is a mystery. Today is a gift. That's why it's called the present!

Friends are a very rare jewel, indeed. They make you smile and encourage you to succeed. They lend an ear, they share a word of praise, and they always want to open their hearts to us.

Enjoy the present!!

As I mentioned before in Chapter 2, during the early years of my real estate career I was privileged to work with another mentor other than Sven Nylund, and his name is Dr. Fred Grosse. My wife and I, along with a group of about five other couples, all very successful Realtors, would meet quarterly to semi-annually with Dr. Grosse to share ideas and in general try to gather the tools and understanding necessary to become more successful.

Dr. Fred emphasized the importance of a few dollar-productive work habits that would help all of us to avoid wasting either time or money or both. As Fred mentions, his philosophy is that "Life Is Primary, And Work Funds Life." Yet as he says, time and again when he visited real estate offices he would see professionals whose income-earning potential could be $300 to $600 or more an hour (when they were doing what they're meant to be doing), instead spending time chatting with colleagues, making copies of contracts and tending to other administrative details. This is not to say that we should not periodically spend time chatting with office colleagues, but we need to remember that each day our primary focus should be focused on activities that result in income.

What Dr. Fred emphasized to all of us in our mentoring group over the years is that many times we would be doing busy work, i.e., any activity that makes us look like we are doing something productive when in actuality we are just filling time doing what someone making $15 an hour could handle. As he said, at the end of a day of busy work, we often would be tired and maybe even depressed. We would get home and would have little, if any, energy to give to our loved ones. We managed to waste another chance to be the best that we could be, and there's nothing left of us to enjoy. We've missed another opportunity to be dollar-productive and have something to show for our time. Dr. Fred gets to the crux of how to avoid this condition. "So what is dollar-productive behavior? It's simple: any activity that earns you income. In the real estate industry, four primary activities qualify: prospect, list, negotiate and sell. If you're doing anything else other than these four activities during the workday, you're not being a REALTOR, and your sales records at the end of the month will reflect it."

Dr. Fred goes on to tell us to start right now to keep a record each day, listing all the activities we have engaged in at work today, hour by hour. We need to include the phone calls to clients and prospective clients, the administrative work, the chat with the friend that stopped by, the drive to put up property signs, everything you can remember. Then, he asks that for the next two weeks, we repeat the ritual every night before we go home.

At the end of the two-week period we need to revisit our hourly records and place a dollar sign next to each dollar-productive activity. As an example, he asks the question: How much did I or will I earn from the two hours of prospecting that I did last Tuesday? It could be $3,000 or even $10,000 or more. What about the coffee break on Friday morning? He says that break should have been spent with a past client, rather than with a colleague in the office.

Dr. Grosse believes we need to be tough and rigorous with ourselves, and we often will be shocked at how many days passed us by with no dollar sign attached to any activity. He believes that typically we as real estate professionals learn that only about five or six hours in a 60-hour work week earned us any income! He says, if that is the case why not combine all six hours into one day, say Monday, and then take the rest of the week off? Or, if you want to double your income, why not consider doing 12 hours of dollar-productive work next week (and taking only Wednesday through Friday off) and then watch the commissions grow.

To me, Dr. Grosse's ideas here were so compelling and logical that I put together a form that I used each day (see Appendix).

If we follow this plan and use it religiously until it becomes a habit and a way of life, just think how much more time we will have to fund life. I highly recommend this approach to real estate sales and, in fact, it applies directly to any business, not just to real estate.

An adjunct to Dr. Fred's dollar-productive activities program is Alan Lakein's program to better manage your time as explained in his book, referenced a few pages back.

The activities listed below in numbers 1-6 summarize Alan's program steps from his book:

1. **List Your Goals – Set Priorities**
    A. What are my long-term goals?
    B. What are my goals for the next six months?
    C. After listing goals – set priorities

I. "A" – high value

II. "B" – medium value

III. "C" – low value

  a. After giving each goal on your list a priority rating, review all the "A's" and select the number 1 priority among that group.

  b. Taking your "A-1" priority, make another list covering the activities necessary to reach your "A-1" goal.

2. Make a Daily "TO DO" List

A. Why a daily list? To be certain that you are moving toward your goals.

B. Update your daily list each day, at the same time, on one sheet of paper.

C. Set priorities on your daily "TO DO" list using the "A, B, C" system above.

D. See what tasks can be delegated.

E. Don't fill every minute with appointments, be flexible.

3. Start with "A's" not with "C's"

A. Get jobs done that are of real value – 80 percent of items on your list are "C's." Spend your time on the other 20% - "A's." Eighty percent of potential sales are found in only the top 20 percent of prospects. Weed out time-consuming "C's" and cultivate the "A's."

4. What is the Best Use of My Time Right Now?

A. Rather than using 10 minutes to get a "C" task done, devote that time to beginning an "A" task – even if it's just organizing it in your own mind.

B. Guideline of importance

   I. CRISIS – personal visit

   II. "A" - phone call

   III. "B" - letter or e-mail

   IV. "C" - if it is not done, no one will ask about it.

C. If too much time is devoted to easy-to-do "C" tasks, it's very possible you will never have time to get to the "A's."

5. Handle Each Piece of Paper Only Once

A. Sort mail/e-mail into three groups using "A, B, C" rating.

   I. Put "C" mail into a drawer and forget about it until you have time to go through it. Clear out the drawer at least once a month.

   II. Take care of "A" and "B" mail. Handle each piece of paper only once. Don't put items aside that will eventually need to be taken care of – do it now, and don't put it down with the thought "I'll do it later." Don't be a paper shuffler.

6. Do It Now!

    A.   Don't put off that "A" task simply because it looks overwhelming.

    B.   "I don't have enough time to tackle something that big today" is not a logical rationale and certainly not an excuse to do nothing.

        I.   When a few extra minutes come up – use that block of time to analyze that "A" task. Don't waste it doing an easy "C" task that doesn't really matter anyway.

        II.   Once an "A" task is analyzed, use extra time to plug away at it until you build enough momentum to finish it up.

        III. Learn to say "No" – don't constantly compromise your time to achieve others' goals.

In my opinion, we should always try to answer the following three questions: (1) should I be doing it? (2) Should I be doing this activity now or later? (3) Should I be doing this activity at all? As one person put it, ask yourself the following question: "What work that I am doing now can be done just as well by someone else if I were sick or on vacation?" Also, as Stephanie Winston says, work with the TRAF technique, the acronym for the four decisions you should make about each piece of paper: you can **T**oss it in the waste basket; **R**efer it; **A**ct on it, or **F**ile it. As she says, the only way to handle your paperwork successfully is TRAF, every single piece of it!

Even though the day can start out quietly and you think you have a great time management plan in place, road-blocks and crises can and will occur. Therefore, it is important to ask yourself several times a day these critical questions:

1. Am I working only on tasks that are necessary and worthwhile?

2. Am I tackling tasks in the order of their priority?

3. Am I finishing tasks within the planned time?

4. Am I delegating enough?

5. Am I grouping smaller tasks in a single work period?

6. Most important, am I fighting interruptions and time wasters?

Our answers here will help us spot unnecessary time wasters and bad habits, such as making unimportant telephone calls, preparing unnecessary reports, and mixing up our priorities.

The following are 45 time management ideas. Some of these ideas have been mentioned earlier in a similar context, but they all have some relevancy.

Time Management Ideas

1. When ordering at a restaurant, order your food and ask for the check at the same time.

2. Use odd times to set appointments, e.g., 9:40 am or 10:10 am. You'll increase the promptness of others.

3. Schedule your time off.

4. Call your sellers on a set day of the week/month.

5. Stand up when you and your guest are finished discussing your business. Also, when a fellow associate or lender or title person comes into your office, immediately stand up and say hello but with a smile on your face. Usually, with both of you standing, business can be transacted quickly and the person can be on his or her way in short order. In my earlier years I would remain seated, the other person would sit down in the chair in front of my desk and I was in for about a 30-minute session, when the business could have been transacted in a matter of a few minutes. Again, this is not to say that we should not periodically spend time with colleagues, but there is a time and place for everything.

6. Have one list, not several.

7. In your idle time, write personal notes (my team and I have a goal of 25 personally written and addressed thank-you notes each week!).

8. Prioritize phone calls.

9. Hold all calls for 30-minute blocks to get things done.

10. Throw things away.

11. Use a separate credit card for business; you then have a list of business expenses for your C.P.A. when preparing your income tax return.

12. Handle each correspondence only once.

13. Have others do detail work and errands.

14. Minimize personal calls at work.

15. Mail things or e-mail; don't deliver personally.

16. Have a GPS system and use it.

17. Use a personal computer and tablet.

18. Use a smartphone.

19. Have a follow-up system in place.

20. Check off items as completed.

21. Set up a breakfast and/or lunch meeting.

22. Wake up and get going 15 minutes early; that results in over an extra hour per week of productive time.

23. Delegate and trust others.

24. Learn to say no.

25. Leave time for the unexpected.

26. Tackle the most difficult tasks first.

27. Constantly weed out prospects.

28. What is the best use of your time NOW?

29. Write reminder notes.

30. Finish one task first.

31. Recap at the end of the day.

32. Intercept people who waste your time.

33. Write down what time to leave for appointments or enter in your smartphone.

34. Go to lunch at 11:30 or 1:00 when the lines are non-existent or shorter.

35. Leave your message if the person you are calling is not in, rather than calling back later.

36. If you must talk to the person, leave a time frame to return your call.

37. When the phone call is completed do not be the first to hang up; if you do the other person will

hear the dial tone, leaving that person thinking you couldn't wait to get off the line.

38. Write things down in the same place, always.

39. Leave your house at the same time daily whenever possible.

40. Work really hard for 30-60 minutes at a time and then take a break (see the next section in this chapter, Energy Management).

41. Put a STOP sign on your desk when you want no interruptions, and keep your door closed during those times.

42. Keep your appointment book or other scheduling vehicle, e.g., your smartphone, with or near you.

43. Take at least one day off per week.

44. Say to yourself daily, "I am more organized than ever before, and I get so much done every day."

45. Real estate is a profession – not your life!

So far, we have been talking about the practical, everyday approach to the utilization of time, and the activities and procedures mentioned should be very useful in our day-to-day life. However, a more philosophical approach to time is also very valuable and generates some deep insights into it.

For example, Albert Einstein said that "creativity is the residue of wasted time." As I mentioned in an earlier chapter, "play" on the surface is a wasted activity, but in reality it lends itself to drawing out our creative nature and actually makes us more fun to be around; after all, we can be too serious!

I received my undergraduate degree in English from Saint John's University, Collegeville, Minnesota. One of my mentors while there was Father Don Talafous, OSB. Father Don is a very wise man, 94 years old and still going strong. He has a daily, free e-mail reflection to which I subscribe. In his July 31, 2016, reflection, Father Don speaks to the frenetic pace that we keep, and to the importance of "being" rather than just always "doing." I am reproducing that reflection here in its entirety.

"After hustling through high school and into the first year of college to take part in every sport known to human beings – well, at least to the school – Sarah asserted herself. She had played softball, basketball, volleyball, hockey; she had rowed and ran. Finally she told the softball coach that she wasn't going to play anymore. He was upset. She thought to herself and tried to explain to him: 'I need time to be human, to think, to pray, to know my friends.' We often talk or hear talk about the good use of time, of our time. But in our society, that sometimes is the equivalent of saying that every moment of time should be taken up with some activity. It begins even in grade school; children and their parents are measured by the number of activities, sports, theater, and music the boy or girl is involved in."

Father Don continues:

"Our use of time is frenetic. We spend so much time 'doing' that there's little left for simply 'being.' Shouldn't there be some time to sit back so as to be

able to look at what we're doing and evaluate it?
Where does this fit into my life or even further: what
is life for? 'What is this life, if full of care, we have no
time to stand and stare?' For adults even breakfast,
lunch and dinner become mere accomplishments
to business. Enjoying another's company, the
conversation, even a meal seems to be a throwback
to some primitive stage in our evolution when people
didn't really know that time was money. Doesn't the
young lady mentioned earlier have the right idea?
Let's hope she's able to enjoy lunch with friends or time
under the trees by a lake without regretting that she's
not at rugby practice."

In his November 9, 2016, reflection, Father Don quotes
Shakespeare in his "Sonnet 60," 'like as the waves make
toward the pebbled shore so do our minutes hasten to
their end.' He continues,

"Time, what a mystery! No matter how long we live,
it remains so incomprehensible. Define it, measure
it as we will, it still eludes our understanding.
Occasions like a death or an anniversary trigger our
uncomprehending musing. A homecoming celebration,
a reunion of any kind does the same.

The same comments are inevitable. 'It seems like
yesterday that I was here. On the other hand, it seems
so far away;' 'So much has changed.' 'So much has
stayed the same.' 'Where has all the time gone?' 'It's
hard to believe it's the second week in November.'
'I'm embarrassed to think about when I last wrote.

*Time goes so fast. Little Susan is now over 2 years
old, but it seems like she was born yesterday.' 'Where
are the snows of yesteryear?' the poet Francois Villon
wrote. 'How fast time goes!' 'I always meant to call for
lunch.' 'Thoughts about time are familiar, universal.
What do we do about them?"*

It is important to see life as it unfolds with its swiftly
passing moments as opportunities to act, to do. The
often-quoted Irish toast goes "May you live all the days
of your life." In this context, living certainly means more
than simply existing. It means we consciously use our
moments, our breath to do something more demanding
than, as Father Don says, "simply watching others get
their exercise or simply taking in what technology offers.
The people around us, from family to friends, especially
benefit from our active interest and love, and I suspect
most of us would feel some pulsating point to life, too, as
a result."

Even the good Lord took time out to rest. "For in six days
the Lord made heaven and earth, the sea, and all that is in
them, and rested on the seventh day; therefore, the Lord
blessed the Sabbath day and made it holy." (Exodus 20).

As Abraham Heschel says in his book, *Sabbath*, "Sabbath
is not for the sake of the weekdays; the weekdays are for
the sake of the Sabbath. It is not an interlude but the
climax of living."

I must confess that in my real estate career I tried my best
to not work on Sunday (the Sabbath), but it was difficult
to put off until Monday presenting that offer that had a

Sunday deadline. However, I do not remember losing a transaction because of not working on Sunday; I think the root cause was my own insecurity THINKING I would lose a deal. In this same regard, I always remembered the survey that was done with kids that I referenced earlier. The kids were asked, "If you had a choice between spending time with your dad, or spending that same time watching TV", 92 percent of the kids said spending time with dad. Then the dads were asked, "What is the average amount of time you spend with your small kids each day?" The dads honestly thought it was about 40 minutes, and the actual time was 37.7 seconds! Time spent with your kids is very valuable and flies by before you know it. Take time for your kids. Just like your dog, they are just wanting to spend time with you.

The following, author unknown, has given me a unique perspective on taking time out of my daily life.

- Take time to work – it is the price of success.
- Take time to think – it is the source of power and perspective.
- Take time to play – it is the secret of youth.
- Take time to do for others – it is in giving that we receive.
- Take time to help and enjoy friends – it is the source of happiness.
- Take time to love – it is the most meaningful sacrament of life.
- Take time to dream – it is the future that gives direction to the present.

- Take time to laugh – it is the best medicine for the body and the soul.

- Take time to travel – it proves that mankind is all one family.

- Take time to plan – it is the secret of being able to have time for the first nine things.

About 20 years ago I read a poem called "The Dash" and it really resonated with me. We are all familiar with seeing the dates of birth and death on tombstones and in the obituary column in the newspapers. The question is: what happened in the dash period from birth to death? How did we use our time?

The Dash
by Linda Ellis

(1934-1998)

I read of a man who stood to speak
At a funeral of a friend.
He referred to the dates on her tombstone,
From the beginning to the end.
He noted that first came her date of birth
And spoke the following date with tears,
But he said what mattered most of all
Was the dash between those years.
For that dash represents all the time
That she spent alive on earth,

And now only those who loved her

Know what that little line is worth.

For it matters not, how much we own;

The cars, the house, the cash,

What matters is how we live and love

And how we spend our dash.

So think about this long and hard...

Are there things you'd like to change?

For you never know how much time is left,

That can still be rearranged.

If we could just slow down enough

To consider what's true and real,

And always try to understand

The way other people feel.

And be less quick to anger,

And show appreciation more

And love the people in our lives

Like we've never loved before.

If we treat each other with respect,

And more often wear a smile

Remembering that this special dash

Might only last a little while.

So, when your eulogy is being read

With your life's actions to rehash...

Would you be proud of the things they say

About how you spent your dash?

I am glad that you are in my life

And part of my dash...laugh long, live long.

Finally, I have two more articles that have really influenced me over the years about the way people that were in ill health and close to dying felt about the life they had lived and the way they had spent their time (I cover this topic in more detail in the chapter on Significance). One is "I'd Pick More Daisies."

I'd Pick More Daisies

If I had my life to live over again, I'd try to make more mistakes next time. I would relax. I would limber up. I would be sillier than I have been this trip. I know of very few things I would take seriously. I would be crazier.

I would be less hygienic. I would climb more mountains swim more rivers and watch more sunsets. I would burn more candles at both ends and then bite into the middles to learn what they are made of. I would eat more ice-cream and less beans. I would have more actual troubles and fewer imaginary ones.

You see, I am one of those people who lives sensibly and sanely, hour after hour, day after day.

Oh, I've had my moments, and if I had to do it over

again, I'd have more of them. In fact, I'd try to have nothing else. Just moments, one after another instead of living so many years ahead of each day. I have been one of those people who never goes anywhere without a thermometer, a hot-water bottle, a gargle, a raincoat, aspirin, and a parachute.

If I had it to do over again, I would go places, and do things and travel lighter than I have.

If I had my life to live over, I would start barefooted earlier in the Spring and stay that way later in the Fall. I would play hooky more, I wouldn't make such good grades except by accident. I would ride on more merry-go-rounds. I'd pick more daisies.

The second article is also reprinted here in full, and was written as an opinion editorial on December 27, 2007, by my friend, Robert Sweeney, editor of *the Villager* magazine, a local newspaper published in the Denver area.

If I Had My Life to Live Over

By Erma Bombeck

I would have invited friends over to dinner even if the carpet was stained, or the sofa faded.

I would have eaten the popcorn in the "good" living room and worried much less about the dirt when someone wanted to light a fire in the fireplace.

I would have taken the time to listen to my grandfather ramble about his youth.

I would never have insisted the car windows be rolled up on a summer day because my hair had just been teased and sprayed.

I would have burned the pink candle sculptured like a rose before it melted in storage.

I would have sat on the lawn with my children and not worried about grass stains.

I would have cried and laughed less while watching television—and more while watching life.

I would have gone to bed when I was sick instead of pretending the earth would go into a holding pattern if I wasn't there for the day.

I would never have bought anything just because it was practical, wouldn't show soil, or was guaranteed to last a lifetime.

Instead of wishing away nine months of pregnancy, I'd have cherished every moment realizing that the wonderment growing inside me was the only chance in life to assist God in a miracle.

When my kids kissed me impetuously, I would never have said, "Later. Now go get washed up for dinner." There would have been more "I love you's" ... and more "I'm sorry's." But mostly, given another shot at life, I would seize every minute ... look at it and really see it ... live it ... and never give it back!

In the final analysis, as the late Bishop Fulton J. Sheen titled his weekly TV program, *Life is Worth Living*, and as the poet and Professor Mary Oliver puts it, "When it's over, I want to say: All my life I was a bride married to amazement. I was a bridegroom, taking the world into my arms. When it's over, I don't want to wonder if I have made something particular, and real. I don't want to find myself sighing and frightened and full of argument. I don't want to end up simply having visited this world."

Energy Management

"Man! I'm bushed!" How many of us have said these words or words similar to them, all too often during the course of our days?

In the preceding segment of this chapter, we spoke about the importance of time management and its proper utilization, and how our earnings are in direct proportion to how effectively we use our time. Most of our efforts should be directed toward getting in front of people that can decide to buy or sell, and that process takes preparation and the expenditure of effort and energy.

This brings us to a discussion of energy management. We need the maximum energy in order to optimally perform the activities necessary to use our time most effectively.

Tony Schwartz and Jim Loehr have teamed up to write their blockbuster, best-selling book called *The Power of Full Engagement*. In this book they state that managing energy, even more so than managing time, is the key to high performance and personal renewal. They say that energy, not time, is our most precious resource, and that "performance, health and happiness are grounded in the skillful management of energy," with full engagement being the energy state that best serves performance. Schwartz and Loehr believe that the following four principles are critical to achieving full engagement and all its benefits:

- Principle 1: Full engagement requires drawing on four separate but related sources of energy: physical, emotional, mental, and spiritual.

- Principle 2: Because energy diminishes both with overuse and with underuse, we must balance energy expenditure with intermittent energy renewal.

- Principle 3: To build capacity we must push beyond our normal limits, training in the same systematic way that elite athletes do.

- Principle 4: Positive energy rituals – highly specific routines for managing energy – are the key to full engagement and sustained high performance.

- Making change that lasts requires a three-step process: Define Purpose, Face the Truth and Take Action.

I have seen in my own life a direct reflection of the misuse of these principles. Early in my real estate sales career

I worked from morning until night, utilizing my energy like it would be going out of style any minute. One Sunday afternoon as I was literally running to make Sunday afternoon mass, I became light-headed and after mass my wife insisted that she take me to the nearby emergency room to get checked out. As it turned out, I was diagnosed with atrial flutter, which meant that I had an irregular heartbeat. As you can well imagine, this scared me to death! Further, they could not get my heart back into sinus rhythm so they had to cardiovert me, i.e., put paddles on me and shock me back into normal rhythm. I cover this situation in more detail in my later chapter on stress.

I wish now that at that time I had the benefit of the information contained in Schwartz and Loehr's book! What I have learned from my experience is several-fold. First, physical energy is fundamental. My daily activities were disjointed and disproportionate. My eating habits were not good at all. I would run out the door in the morning with a banana in hand and that would become my breakfast! I would usually eat a little lunch while at my desk. I can recall that around 4 p.m. or so my energy was flagging badly, so I would grab a handful of cookies that seemed to be available most days in the office lunchroom. So my energy would then spike and crash, depending upon how long I had gone without eating and what sort of sugary snacks I ate. As a result, I would get tired and often find myself dozing off. Many times I would have an early-evening listing appointment and was just not on my game. I couldn't wait to get home and have my big evening meal, for which I sat down around 8 or 9 p.m. Then, of course, I was so tired I would head to bed, and day after day would not get any exercise.

I also found that the primary barriers to effective performance for me were impatience and irritability. I was not the best person at a stop light if the driver in front of me didn't move out right away when the light turned from red to green. Also, my low energy made me more vulnerable to negative emotions.

Again, as I look back I also was experiencing poor focus; in other words, I found it difficult to stay focused mentally at work. I was easily distracted and was more inefficient than before.

Indeed, sadly, my life was out of balance. Being a fairly religious man, I took comfort in the Serenity Prayer, "God grant me the serenity to accept the things I cannot change; the courage to change the things I can; and the wisdom to know the difference."

I was spending too much of my energy worrying about people and situations over which I had no control, and I began to realize that I was a lot better off to concentrate my energy on those situations that I could influence. I began to realize that I had a pretty fragile sense of self-worth. From my readings I remembered the classic Greek saying of "know thyself." I realized that I was out of balance and needed to correct this issue. I began to reflect on why I was so driven to succeed and started to realize that the tragedy of our little boy, Eric, going into that deep coma for 14 years (discussed in Chapter 1) and remaining in it until he passed away, may have pushed me disproportionately hard into my work just so I could keep my sanity.

I was really searching for meaning and looking hard at the question: is the life I am living worth what I am giving up to have it? My research was showing me that there was almost no correlation between my income level, which was terrific, and happiness.

I also prided myself on getting maybe four or five hours of sleep each night. I felt sleep was a fairly useless activity and took me away from sales. Boy! Was I off track! I started to learn that physical energy is my foundation and if I neglected it, it showed up in my inability to manage my emotions. I found that indeed adequate sleep was the very foundation of my physical energy. As Tony Schwartz so succinctly states it, "No single behavior more fundamentally influences our effectiveness in waking life. Sleep deprivation takes a powerful toll on our health, our emotional well-being, and our cognitive functioning. Finally, spiritual energy is the uniquely powerful source of energy we derive from deeply held values and a clear sense of purpose beyond our self-interest, which we embody in our everyday behaviors."

So, energy management is equally important if not more important than time management, although both are important to achieving a well-rounded and successful life. We need to feel well physically, mentally, and emotionally, otherwise our business and our relationships with our co-workers and our clients will suffer.

As Jamie Nowak, Director of Corporate Development and Training for Buffini and Company, which is the largest training organization for real estate salespeople in the world (see also my chapter on Goal-Setting), states, "How you expend, invest and replenish your energy is the key to high performance in business and life." According to her, the following are Energy Drainers, Energy Givers, and Energy Sustainers. This information is taken from her article in a 2013 Buffini and Company magazine.

Energy Drainers

- **Fear and worry**: They sap your energy and steal your motivation; focus on what you can actually control and encourage your agents to do the same.

- **Indecision**: It paralyzes you and derails your progress.

- **Drama**: We're drawn to it, but it distracts us from what we need to do while trapping us in a negative state of mind.

- **Physical condition**: Poor nutrition and lack of exercise and/or sleep negatively affect performance.

- **Lack of direction**: Aim at nothing and you'll hit it with amazing accuracy.

Energy Givers

- **Positive associations**: Surround yourself with positive, supportive people. Pay attention to whom you hire and whom you keep as an associate. Be selective!

- **Mental intake**: Read, listen to and watch positive media and materials. Facilitate "Peak Producers" in your organization a few times a year (Note: "Peak Producers" is an excellent training program offered by Buffini and Company). This program is full of excellent strategies and tactics on building and sustaining an incredible business. It provides you and your agents action steps to help you focus on the most important priorities and habits in your business.

- **Take care of yourself:** Eat nutritious food, work out regularly, and get 7-8 hours of sleep each night.

- **Align your values:** Invest time each day in the most important people and activities in your life and business. This will give you peace of mind.

- **Write goals:** Focus on the things you want for your life and create an action plan to achieve them.

Energy Sustainers

Once you get energy working for you, how do you keep it going strong?

- **Track your progress:** Writing down the important activities you've accomplished (e.g., recruiting, calls you've made, training classes you've taught, distances you've run) is a good way to see how far you've come and offers encouragement along the way. It also reveals any course corrections that might be necessary.

- **Create visual anchors:** Create a goal board for yourself and have your agents/staff do so as well – this will help everyone keep their eye on the prize!

- **Be consistent:** The following is a three-step formula to achieving consistency with good habits and disciplines: First, prioritize. If everything is a priority, then nothing is. Make a list of your top three business and personal activities and/or people each day; differentiate your "need-to-dos" from your "like-to-dos." Second, set boundaries. Have a beginning and end time to your workday, take at least one day off each week, and turn your phone and e-mail off after 6 or 7 p.m. Third, time block. Take your list of priorities and schedule them first.

- **Take a break:** In this fast-paced industry, especially as a leader, it's crucial to take time away from the business. Instead of just going and going with no end in sight, have the mindset of a sprinter. Work hard for a predetermined period of time, take a rest, then repeat. Give yourself and your family breaks to look forward to throughout the year. This will rejuvenate everyone and make you much more productive too! Tip: schedule these breaks first, and then book everything else around them.

- **Be accountable:** Being held accountable by a coach, trusted mentor or peer partner is essential for achieving worthwhile goals in all areas of life. In fact, accountability is responsible for a large percentage of all achievement. When you know you're being held accountable to certain activities and goals by someone you respect, you'll always work harder to get things done. Harness that power!

And when the whole day is lost to the urgent, the noise, or other circumstances, as sometimes happens when you're a leader in this industry, nothing takes the place of perseverance. Get up the next day and start again.

Invest 15 minutes in the morning to think, pray or look at your goals. Put a positive CD on in the car or walk for 20 minutes at lunch.

Keep going. Protect yourself and your priorities and push through those painful times when you want to quit. Remember why you're doing what you're doing and keep a daily record of small victories that you can draw on when you feel all is lost. This will give you the important fuel you need to continue moving toward your best life. And this also sets a fantastic example to the people you lead that this business can be full of opportunity, profits, balance, and great clients if you'll stoke the fires of your energy by taking care of your important asset: You.

Wise old Ben Franklin sums it up pretty well when he says, "Energy and persistence conquer all things."

5.

How I Deal With Comparison, Fear and Worry, and Stress

Comparison — Helpful or Harmful?

I **HAVE BEEN THINKING** long and hard about how to adequately cover the comparison topic in this chapter so that it says what I want it to say. I think the topic is as meaningful as any I have discussed, but also is a bit challenging to properly articulate.

I think the first place to explore comparison is with the dictionary definition, specifically, the definition in The Random House Dictionary of the English Language. There we find comparison defined as "The function of an adverb or adjective that is used to indicate degrees of superiority or inferiority in quality, quantity or intensity."

From the day we are born we are being compared. Our parents compare us with the kids of other parents, e.g., when did we first roll over on our own, when did we start crawling, when did we take our first halting steps – the list goes on and on. As we grow older our parents tell us when these milestones occurred and compare them to those of little Johnny down the street. As we get a bit older we play tee-ball, and we can see which kid hits the ball better and more frequently.

Not only are we compared to others, but we are compared to ourself and how we shape up at any given time.

I remember my parents telling me as I was growing up to "stick my shoulders back and stand up straight." They did not want me to grow up to be hunched over. I can remember finding it difficult to do as they asked and so I was alternating, time-wise, from being accepted and not being accepted, depending upon how straight – shoulders back – I stood!

In grade school and high school I participated in all sports, but was especially talented in baseball. I remember being elated that I was selected to have a one-day tryout with the old Milwaukee Braves. I remember being so excited that the powers that be compared my potential and talent with other baseball hopefuls, finding it to be somewhat high in baseball-playing potential; however, long story short, that was as far as the "tryout" had gotten. Nevertheless, I always felt so good that my comparison to other hopefuls kept me in the mix for a bit longer than most.

Then, when I got through high school I found myself starting on a straight-commission sales career. Our family had virtually no money, so I knew if I was going to go to college it was on me to make it happen. I started selling cookware, cutlery, china, and flatware. Again I found myself being compared by my sales production. The rankings would be listed every month, and I would always rush to see how I ranked compared to the other salespeople around the country. My last year with American Salesmasters, mentioned in Chapter 2, I ended up with my production ranking me as the number 2 salesperson out of 85 of my colleagues (or was it "competitors?"), nationwide. Early in my real estate career I would often receive trophies, and in 1976 I was billed as the number 1 residential real estate salesperson in the United States by *Success Magazine.*

Obviously in order to reach the accomplishments noted above, I had to work hard and effectively, and I did so. However, as year after year I received those awards, I must confess that I grew afraid that I would not be able to keep up my sales pace and continue receiving those awards. I had a love-hate relationship going. I enjoyed the accolades but was not sure how long I could sustain the hard work and diligence necessary to keep going and make the number of sales required to maintain my position as the number 1 residential real estate salesperson in my company, in Colorado, and in the United States.

As my family was growing, I started to feel increasingly guilty about the amount of time I was spending away from my wife and kids. I knew I should be spending more time with them but the drive for more sales continued to take precedence!

In the Appendix, I have attached two hand-written notes that my daughter, Kate, gave me when she was a little girl over thirty-seven years ago! They will show my readers how much she was often desperately searching for my time, attention, and proof that I cared about her. To this day I regret that she felt compelled to address those notes to me. She undoubtedly was comparing the time and attention that her friends were receiving from their fathers and quite rightly wanted some of that attention for herself.

I must say that one of my saving graces during those years was the private Ports-of-Call Travel Club, mentioned earlier, headquartered in Denver. As a family we would sign up for short trips to neat destinations like Eleuthera and other warm-weather places. Thank God that I had the one-on-ones with my kids that these trips afforded my wife and me!

I will be the first to admit that comparing ourselves with others keeps us Realtors on our toes and helps us strive to do better. My constant working hard to better myself and increase my sales has enabled me to provide very well financially for my family; but as Doris Mortman says, "Until you make peace with who you are, you'll never be content with what you have."

The key is to take the best of the results of comparison and try to understand and minimize the negative aspects.

In my attempts to focus on the positive aspects of my uniqueness, here is what has helped me. First, I have begun to realize how very unique and special we human beings are. With all the billions of humans that have walked and will be walking the face of the earth, none of us are totally like any other! This in itself should keep us from negatively comparing ourselves to others! Our human brain is about 2 percent of our body weight and consumes about 20 to 30 percent of our body's energy. The human brain has about 100 billion neurons and 1 quadrillion connections. No doubt exists that each of us is totally one of a kind!

As Walt Disney said, "The more you like yourself, the less you are like anyone else, which makes you unique." It is really gratifying and comforting to know that we are unique and one of a kind. There never has been anyone like me or you in the world before and there never will be again. My friend Robert White has written a great book called *Living an Extraordinary Life.* As he says, many of us are sick and tired of our nagging blemishes, of the way we look and the way our life is, especially when we compare ourselves to many other people. But, as he further says, what can we do about it? According to him, we have two choices:

1. Continue to resist who we are, and fight to eliminate your shortcomings.

2. Stop the resistance. Accept your uniqueness, focus on your greatness, and learn to love who you are. You are the source of all you experience. You are a gift to your family, your company, your neighborhood, your community, your nation, and to the world.

Robert says that we need to get rid of the "I'm not enough" belief, and the following are some of its common versions:

I have nothing to contribute.

I'm not important.

I'm a failure.

I don't deserve to have the best.

I'm not lovable.

Everyone knows more than me.

I can't because I'm not creative.

I can't because I'm too shy.

I can't because I'm lazy.

I can't because I'm afraid.

I can't because I didn't go to college.

I can't because I'm just like my father/mother.

I can't because I'm not like my father or mother or Julia Roberts or Mel Gibson.

There's not enough time.

Life is a never-ending struggle.

I'll never have enough money.

I can't trust myself.

People are all bad.

People are all better than me.

I can't because I'm not strong enough.

I can't because I'm not assertive.

I'm too young.

I'm too old.

My nose or buttocks or hips or _____ are too big.

My breasts or penis or _____ are too small.

I'm unattractive.

People always rip me off.

I can't trust men.

I can't trust women.

I can't be happy.

I can't talk to people.

We need to get rid of these self-limiting beliefs stemming from the most common belief in the world, namely, that the real me is not lovable, that I AM NOT ENOUGH. As Dr. Nathaniel Branden, Author of *The Six Pillars of Self-Esteem*, says, "of all the judgments we pass in life, none is as important as the one we pass on ourselves." Joan Didion says that "to have that sense of one's intrinsic worth which constitutes self-respect is potentially to have everything."

The famous singer, Whitney Houston, in her song "Greatest Love of All," written by Linda Creed and Michael Massur, sings that song so well with these words: "Because the greatest love of all is happening to me. I've found the greatest love of all inside of me. The greatest love of all is easy to achieve. Learning to love yourself, it is the greatest love of all."

In a nutshell, the belief that I'm not as good as other people, that the real me is unlovable, is the most common belief in the world.

In his May 28, 2016, daily reflection, Father Don Talafous, OSB, whom I also referenced in the chapter on Time Management, says,

> *"One of the terrible truths that marks the end of our innocence is learning that not everyone is going to like us. And, in many cases, there is nothing we can do about it. For legitimate reasons or not some don't like our looks, our behavior, our traits (so lovable to others), the way we talk or walk or hold a cup or smile or laugh. If we've been brought up in a loving family, among tolerant friends and neighbors, it's a shock to realize that no amount of goodwill and sincerity on our part is going to alter the indifference or antagonism of some. We'll often have to work with these people or in close proximity at least; while at our first job we might even share a house with some who feel that way."*

Father Don continues,

> *"There are, of course, cases where our charm or sincerity does win over others and people who at first locked horns end up as friends, even husband and wife. More self-knowledge, some analysis of our own self might help. We will probably discover if we're honest that we have an inexplicable antipathy toward certain people. We will probably not even be*

able to say who or what irritates us. This is where the practice of some ordinary politeness can be helpful. By it we practice good will and respect toward all those we encounter. If we were expected to like everyone equally, we'd have a terrible time settling on a life partner; there would be no difference between people. The prickliness we feel in human relations, whether rooted in ourselves or others, is simply a sign of life's imperfection. Self-knowledge can teach us tolerance and even understanding of those who seem so uncongenial to us. However, the good news is that a deep and lasting self-love is possible for all of us."

Ok, you might say, it's easier said than done. Most of us do compare and many of us find ourselves coming out on the short end of the stick. In my Goal-Setting chapter, I spoke about Rabbi Harold Kushner's book, *How Good Do We Have to Be?* I would like to develop here more fully the train of thought expressed in that book.

I am a Christian, more specifically a Roman Catholic, and the ideas expressed by Rabbi Kushner have helped me tremendously. Many of us who have been raised as Catholics have issues with guilt and not being perfect. I always thought I had to be perfect, and then finally realized that perfection was an illusion. I referenced Rabbi Kushner in my chapter on Goal-Setting, and what he says in my opinion is so powerful that it bears referencing here again!

"A lot of misery could be traced to this one mistaken notion: we need to be perfect for people to love us and we forfeit that love if we ever fall short of perfection." Rabbi

Kushner says that the source of many of our anxieties is the notion "that we were supposed to be perfect, and that we could expect others to be perfect because we needed them to be, which leaves us feeling constantly guilty and perpetually disappointed."

The person who claims to be perfect and without flaw or defect, is claiming to be God. As Rabbi Kushner says, "God may be disappointed in some of the things we do; he is never disappointed in who we are, fallible people struggling with the implications of knowing Good and Evil."

Rabbi Kushner tells the story of when he visited a young minister at Johns Hopkins medical center in Baltimore; the minister was dying of AIDS. Like me, he told Rabbi Kushner that when he was young, he thought he had to be perfect for people to love him, and his parents gave him that message. He tried so hard to be perfect, so that his parents, his teachers, and God himself would love him. What he told Rabbi Kushner was that he finally learned that God knows what I'm like and he does not hate me, so I don't have to hate myself. God knows what I've done, and he loves me anyway. "You don't have to be perfect. Just do your best, and God will accept you as you are. Don't expect your children to be perfect. Love them for their faults, for their trying and stumbling, even as our Father in Heaven loves us."

I have learned that the greatest thing you can leave your children is the memory that God loves them just as they are and accepts them and forgives them. According to the great billionaire investor, Warren Buffett, "The most important job you have is to be a teacher to your children."

As someone once told me and as I have referenced several times throughout this book, "beyond a reasonable discipline, be good to yourself." If nothing short of perfection will permit us to stand before God, then none of us will, because none of us are perfect. One of the best sayings that has helped me with this issue is the following: "God loves us just as we are and accepts us and forgives us."

In comparing humans and apes, Charles Darwin was asked if there was still anything totally unique about human beings. He answered that "man is the only animal that blushes." What I believe he means here is that humans are the only creatures capable of recognizing the gap between what they are and what they can be expected to be, and of being embarrassed by that gap.

In its essence, the emotion of guilt is feeling bad for what you have done or not done, while shame is feeling bad for who you are, measured against some standard of perfection or acceptability. The distinction is crucial because we can atone for the things we have done more easily than we can change who we are. But human nature being what it is, we move so easily from one to the other. We hear criticism of something we have done and translate it into a comment about what sort of person we are. We assume it is our worth as a person, not just our behavior, that is being judged and found wanting. The school child assumes that his report card is evaluating him as a person, not just his spelling and math performance. So, a bad grade means "I am bad" and a failing grade means

"I am a failure." A youngster overhears his or her parents saying, "She's so shy around other children," or, "He's so much shorter than other boys his age," and feels a sense of shame for having disappointed the parents.

In further examination of the emotion of shame, Dr. Joyce Brothers wrote a great article in the February 27, 2005 issue of Parade Magazine. She says that while some shame can be good, too much can be bad and detrimental for us. Here is her comparison of good shame and bad shame:

GOOD SHAME VERSUS BAD SHAME

Good shame can lead to self-discovery and growth and can nurture and protect. It:

- Gives you new insight about yourself.

- Encourages you to make improvements.

- Expands your value system.

- Makes you more sensitive to others.

- Makes you want to elevate the culture around you.

Bad shame humiliates and makes you feel bad about the way you look or feel. It:

- Attacks you as a person.

- Eats away at self-esteem.

- Evokes an angry response.

- Gets passed along to your children.

- Leaves you feeling helpless.

As Dr. Brothers further says, the root of the word "shame" means "to cover". A certain amount of shame can be good. "In many respects shame seems to be even more powerful than guilt, though the two emotions are certainly linked. Guilt is the feeling that you have done something wrong, shame is the feeling that there's something wrong about you."

Essentially, guilt feelings should be attached to the deed, not to the doer of the deed. God indeed does accept us as we are, and with that acceptance comes the process of healing our shame. When we know that we are acceptable and lovable is when we will be able to change the things we don't like about ourselves.

In the bible, Romans 12:3, translated into down-to-earth, everyday language, really says it well: "Let's just go ahead and be what we were made to be, without enviously or pridefully comparing ourselves with each other, or trying to be something we aren't." Dr. Hans Selye, the great expert on stress, says that emotional stress is caused by trying to be something you are not.

Along this same line of reasoning, I once went to a seminar where each of the attendees was given a mask when they checked in. They asked us to wear those masks during the entire course of the seminar, and they were used to emphasize the "false self," the tendency to not show people who we really are, and that had a big impact on me. What they were trying to prove is that it takes a lot of energy to put that awkward mask on each day and be what we think other people want us to be. It is rooted in the desire to please everyone and to be all things to all people.

That is especially true of people in sales. We want to appeal to the maximum number of people in order that the maximum number of people will be attracted to us and buy from us. As one person that I know said, "We wear masks for a good portion of our lives." Along this same line of reasoning, Father Pat Dolan, pastor of Most Precious Blood Catholic Church in Denver, Colorado, said in his January 20, 2016, sermon, "Too many people want to be liked for who they are not, rather than having others know who they really are." He further says that when we are being caught off guard we are really our most authentic self, with no masks on and being the person that God intended us to be, being totally vulnerable, and enjoying the process.

How liberating it is for our psyche to be secure enough in ourselves to go about our lives without the constraint of putting on our daily mask, i.e., to be so secure in our "worthiness" that we realize, according to Robert White, referenced earlier, that "everything we enjoy in society is a direct result of the accumulated learning derived from millions of mistakes. No mistakes, no progress. Yet we still look at a mistake as embarrassing, wrong, an act bordering on sin. If you're making mistakes, it means you're doing new things, taking risks, stretching yourself. You're growing, learning. And is not the journey, the experience – not the destination – what life is all about?"

According once again to Father Don, this time in his September 28, 2016 reflection, the source of dissatisfaction upon comparison is the vice of ENVY. Envy has been defined as "sorrow over someone else's good." As he says:

> *"We make ourselves miserable because someone else has some good. We're sad because mom pampers that shiftless brother, because John got a promotion, because that smiling and even-tempered Cindy has so many friends. Envy is called a capital sin from the Latin word for 'head' because, like the other six sins, it is the source from which other sins arise. Left to grow, envy leads to backbiting, theft, even murder."*

He further says that in the novel, *Billy Budd*, the seaman who envied "the good looks, cheery health and frank enjoyment of life" of the hero eventually meets an untimely death. Envy makes us think that because someone else has some good, we are diminished. Envy doesn't inspire us to imitate them but to hope that they will fail. Under the influence of envy, we are "unable to admire, respect or be grateful for what is nobler or lovelier or greater than ourselves." The answer to envy must be, one, to value what we are, to rejoice in it and use it well. And secondly, to rejoice in the good in others: their accomplishments, artistry, their smiles and laughter. Worship is a school where we can be taught a habit of esteeming what is admirable, good, and appealing. In weekly praise of God we might learn to approach our fellow human beings with similar praise. We might say more often, "Wow" or "Magnificent" or "Beautiful" or simply "Thank you."

Some people do not want to experience the personal torment that can go along with constantly being on the comparison rollercoaster, and that is at least partially why many people just strive for conformity. If they conform as much as possible they live a rather dull life, but they don't get in the comparison, often competitive mode, where they start to stand out, whether positively or negatively. However, on balance, the price we pay for conformity can be very negative and debilitating.

As Robert White, referenced earlier several times, says,

"We stop risking for fear of making mistakes, fear of not fitting in, fear of being embarrassed or humiliated by saying the wrong thing. Our instinctive joy and boundless enthusiasm are replaced by playing it safe and looking good. Our spontaneity deserts us, and with it much of our natural creativity. Predictability replaces passion. We learn to reveal very little of who we really are and what we really feel. We sell the richness of our passionate birthright for the security of this burdensome thing called our image. It weighs us down like a suit of medieval armor, restricting our every move, sapping our vitality and aliveness. We wander through life on automatic pilot, controlled by the need to live up to the false image that we invented."

In her best-selling book, *Daring Greatly*, author Brené Brown quotes Theodore Roosevelt's speech delivered at the Sorbonne in Paris, France, on April 23, 1910. That speech is as follows:

"It is not the critic who counts; not the man who

points out how the strong man stumbles, or where the doer of deeds could have done them better. The credit belongs to the man who is actually in the arena, whose face is marred by dust and sweat and blood; who strives valiantly ... who at the best knows in the end the triumph of high achievement, and who at worst, if he fails, at least fails while daring greatly."

The phrase "daring greatly" at the end of the speech forms the basis of Brown's book. She says to be truly authentic, to remove our masks, so to speak, we cannot spend our lives waiting until we are perfect or bulletproof before we walk into the arena, whether it be a new relationship, an important listing presentation or a difficult family conversation.

We in the real estate sales profession are especially in the arena, as it were, every single day. We are not in the bleachers or on the sidelines. We are constantly face-to-face with a seller who affirms and ratifies us by listing their home with us, or by a buyer who decides to work with another Realtor after we have spent many hours working with that buyer.

Brown says we need to get into our arenas every single day from a position of vulnerability, of engaging life with courage, to show up and let ourselves be seen, to strive for "worthiness" and whole-hearted living. We should not be living in the "scarcity," "never enough" mentality, but rather realizing that even though each of us lives every day with our frailties and imperfections, we are totally unique, and that what we know does matter, but who we are matters even more.

So, in summary, "comparison" can be a debilitating, negative harmful condition, but it can also be the stimulus for growth and fulfillment in the real estate sales profession, or in any profession for that matter. With growth comes competition both from others and from our own self. We need to realize that we are imperfect beings living in an imperfect world, but a world that on balance contains good people all trying to do the best they can to live out their lives with some sense of dignity, purpose, and hope. Pope Francis declared 2016 as the year of mercy. In layman's language he asked all of us to give each other a break and, as I mentioned earlier, beyond a reasonable discipline be good to ourselves and to others. We are all in this together, especially in these unsettling COVID-19 times, and we need to be more kind to ourselves and to others. In doing so, both we and our fellow men and women can strip off the shackles of our masks occasioned by fear, insecurity, and low self-esteem, and be the fully authentic, totally unique individuals that God created us to be. Only when this is achieved can we wake each day and say with 100 percent conviction, as quoted in the Psalms – "This is the day that the Lord has made, let us rejoice and be glad in it."

Fear and Worry

How many times have we said, or have we heard other people say, "Man! I am worrying myself to death?" We worry way too much! Psychologists tell us that indeed we are worrying ourselves to death! Dr. Walter Alverez of the Mayo Clinic has been quoted as saying, "We little realize the number of human diseases that are begun by or are affected by worry."

We have a worry epidemic on our hands in the United States and, for that matter, throughout the world. Consider these facts: the American public consumes 19 million sleeping tablets each night, and 11 million pounds of aspirin per year, the equivalent of 50 headaches per head; more than half of all the hospital beds in the United States are occupied by patients with non-physical problems. We have a suicide occurring every three minutes, and approximately 50 percent of all marriages end in divorce. We do have a serious problem here in the United States, so what can we do about it?

The dictionary defines worry as follows: "To feel uneasy or anxious, to fret, torment ourselves with or suffer from disturbing thoughts." The word "worry" comes from the Anglo-Saxon verb "wyrgan," which means to choke or to strangle. Isn't that what happens to us when we worry? So how do we overcome worry as it chokes off our creativity and effectiveness, robs us of our health, and in extreme cases, robs us of our very life itself?

One of the best books I have ever read to help me keep my worry issues in check is Dale Carnegie's book, *How to Stop Worrying and Start Living*. This book was copyrighted in 1944 and is still a classic and a best-seller on the subject. In that book, Dale gives us some excellent methods of dealing with worry, as follows:

The law of averages technique: Carnegie relates that in a study of things that people worried about, the following results occurred: 40 percent of the things that people worry about never even happen; 30 percent are things in the past and that cannot be changed; 12 percent are needless worries about our health; 10 percent are petty, miscellaneous worries; and only 8 percent are real, legitimate worries. The point here is that if we were playing major league baseball and could bat successfully 92 percent of the time, we would be the player of the year and receive all sorts of awards. And yet that is exactly where we are at with the things that we worry about, e.g., losing a listing to our main competitor, or having our buyer work with another Realtor. The vast majority of these types of worries never even take place, and those few that do occur are neither as frequent nor as upsetting as we anticipate that they are going to be.

The famous writer and pundit, the late Earl Nightingale, referenced earlier several times, says that the trick is to winnow the 8 percent from the 100 percent. He says that this is where being well adjusted, or at least better adjusted, helps. As we get older, one of the great compensations is that we tend to worry less, and that we learn from ourselves what the experts tell us: that just about all of our concerns solve themselves one way or the other in the long run.

Getting back to Mr. Carnegie, he gives us another method of dealing with worry. He says that we should place a "stop-loss" on the things that we worry about. Just like in a stock purchase, we believe the stock will go up in value or we would not have purchased it. However, in the unlikely event that it takes a sharp drop, we do wish to protect ourselves from a large loss. Therefore when we buy the stock, we place a sell order at, e.g., 15 percent below what we paid for it; we then know that the most we can lose is 15 percent of what we paid for the stock. The point for us as Realtors is for us to also place a "stop-loss" on worrying about an undesirable situation that may occur or has occurred.

The above two methods of dealing with worry have helped me a lot. Also, Rabbi Harold Kushner's book, *Conquering Fear,* has been helpful as well. Fear is what results in worry, and in fact, Rabbi Kushner says, somewhat tongue-in-cheek, there ought to be an 11th commandment – "Don't be Afraid."

As I mentioned, I am a Christian and a practicing Catholic, and with the ups and downs that I have experienced in my real estate career, I have taken, and continue to take, great comfort in the quotes from the bible about how to face worry and fear and not to be afraid of it. Some of the quotes that have been most compelling, comforting, and helpful for me have been the following.

Trusting in Providence: Then he said to his disciples,

- *"That is why I am telling you not to worry about your life and what you are to eat, nor about your body and how you are to clothe it. For life means more than food, and the body more than clothing. Think of the ravens. They do not sow or reap; they have no storehouses and no barns; yet God feeds them. And how much more are you worth than the birds! Can any of you, for all his worrying, add a single cubit to his span of life? If the smallest things, therefore, are outside your control, why worry about the rest? Think of the flowers; they never have to spin or weave; yet I assure you, not even Solomon in all his regalia was robed like one of these. Now if that is how God clothes the grass in the field which is there today and thrown into the furnace tomorrow, how much more will he look after you, you men of little faith! But you, you must not set your hearts on things to eat and things to drink; nor must you worry. It is the pagans of this world who set their hearts on all these things. Your Father well knows you need them. No; set your hearts on his kingdom, and these other things will be given you as well. There is no need to be afraid, little flock, for it has pleased your Father to give you the kingdom." Luke 12:22-32.*

- *"And I tell you, ask and you will receive, seek and you will find; knock and the door will be opened to you." Luke 11:9.*

- *"Trust in the Lord forever! For the Lord is an eternal rock." Isaiah 26:4.*

- *"Therefore, I tell you, all that you ask for in prayer, believe that you will receive it and it shall be yours." Mark 11:24.*

- *"I should like you to be free of anxieties." 1 Corinthians 7:32.*

- *"I command you: be strong and steadfast! Do not fear nor be dismayed for the Lord, your God is with you wherever you go." Joshua 1:9.*

- *"There is no need to worry; but if there is anything you need, pray for it. Asking God for it with prayer and thanksgiving, and that peace of God, which is so much greater than we can understand, will guard your hearts and your thoughts, in Christ Jesus." Philippians 4:6-7.*

- *"I can do everything through Christ, who gives me strength." Philippians 4:13.*

When I have had a particularly tough day, have lost what I thought was a sure listing, or when I have had a deal that is falling apart due to a rough inspection, I pull out these passages and read them over and over. It really helps to calm me down and give me the proper perspective on the situation.

In fact, more than 80 times in the bible God tells us not to be afraid. He says it to Abraham, to Isaac, to Jacob, to Moses, the list goes on and on. In the New Testament, Jesus on many occasions tells his disciples not to be afraid, and the angel's first words to Mary are "Do not be afraid."

Rabbi Kushner's tongue-in-cheek "11th commandment, Don't Be Afraid," is meant to keep us from missing out on many of the blessings of life that are accessible only to those who are able to face their fears, see them clearly, and stare them down. As he says, "Don't be afraid of being afraid. Our goal should never be the denial of fear but the mastery of fear, the refusal to let fear keep us from living fully and happily."

In the final paragraph of his book, *Conquering Fear*, Rabbi Kushner says "I confront my fears with the knowledge that failure and rejection are not fatal, that the people who love me, love me for who I am and for what I stand for at my best, not for what I achieve, and I keep reminding myself that hope and courage are the will of God. I leave you with the words of the philosopher – psychologist William James, 'These, then are my last words to you: Be not afraid of life. Believe that life is worth living and your belief will help create the fact.'"

In addition to the points referenced so far in this chapter, several other ways of dealing with fear and worry have been helpful to me.

I have noticed that my tension grows when I allow negative mental habits of thinking to enter my mind. Instead of focusing on the positive, I focus on such negative thoughts as "they aren't going to make an offer," or "they won't qualify," or, all too often, "the out-of-towner has not returned my several calls and has probably hooked up with a competing Realtor." In my opinion, these are the "what if" lists that we need to fight constantly. For example, "What if I lose my job?" "What if my spouse/ significant other dies?" "What if my car breaks down?" "What if I fail at home-schooling my children?" "What if I get a serious illness?"

So, what are some of the ways to overcome these negative thoughts? I think one of the most powerful ways to do so is to simply accept myself instead of to constantly compare myself to others (see my chapter on Comparison). Dr. Smiley Blanton, author of *Love or Perish*, says that lack of self-esteem (low self-image) is probably the most common emotional ailment he's asked to treat.

I have tended to take myself too seriously and to hold myself to too high a standard. I have to continually remind myself of the advice given to me by an old friend years ago and as mentioned previously, namely that, "beyond a reasonable discipline be good to myself." I need to continually remind myself to not be so hard on myself and on others, and to cut myself some slack and show myself some grace. As H. Jackson Brown Jr. says, "Strive for excellence, not perfection."

Other techniques that have been helpful for me to put fear and worry in their place are to have specific but realistic goals (touched on in my Goal-Setting chapter), and to keep a positive mental attitude. As Abraham Lincoln said many times, "Every man is about as happy as he makes up his mind to be." It really boils down to mind discipline.

In sales we are always susceptible to being rejected, and for so long in my real estate career I took it personally if, e.g., someone listed with another Realtor, especially if that person was a good friend or neighbor. However, over the years I have learned that the seller is not rejecting me but rather is rejecting my proposition, i.e., rejecting my request that they list their home with me. I began to realize that rejection is part and parcel of our life as a salesperson, and therefore that sales individual who has the most rejections but at the same time does not let them get him or her down will be the most successful! I have learned to plan on making as many as eight good-old-fashioned mistakes a day, and to just look at them as learning opportunities while at the same time keeping my attitude positive.

However, as the famous columnist, Harvey Mackay, quoted previously, says, "If you don't learn from your mistakes, then there's no sense making them." I am reminded of Thomas Edison who was having a tough time inventing the lightbulb. His friends would ask him, "Aren't you getting down in the dumps now that you still have failed for the 100th time?" Of course, Edison's answer, in his indomitable, positive style is as follows: "Gentlemen, I have not failed for the 100th time, but rather, I have just found out 100 ways that it can't be done – I am just that much closer to the answer!"

Another mindset that I have found helpful is to not expect gratitude from people because when they do not thank me, I find it to be very difficult on my psyche. Along this same line of thinking, years ago I heard the following quote:

"I am going to meet people today who talk too much, people who are selfish, egotistical and ungrateful. But I would not be surprised or disappointed, for I couldn't imagine a world without such people."

What really got me was who made this statement and when he made it; it was Marcus Aurelius, the great Roman Emperor, who lived from 121 to 180 A.D.!

When I first heard this, it really hit me that this whole mindset and situation has been around for ages, and in a funny way this knowledge gave me, and continues to give me, some comfort. The point is, ingratitude was prevalent thousands of years ago, and it continues to be common now! So we should treat those people like gold who do show gratitude to us and to others.

Finally, I periodically would see myself falling into a "woe is me" mindset, and when that starts to rear its ugly head, I pull out and read the following poem, author unknown, that has been with me for years:

Lord, Forgive Me When I Whine

Today upon a bus I saw a lovely girl with golden hair.

I envied her as she seemed so gay and wished I were as fair.

When suddenly she rose to leave I saw her hobble down the aisle.

She had one leg and wore a crutch, but as she passed, a smile.

Oh God, forgive me when I whine, I have two legs, the world is mine.

I stopped to buy some candy, the lad who sold it had such charm.

I talked with him, he seemed so glad.

If I were late it would do no harm.

And as I left, he said to me "I thank you, you have been so kind,

It's so nice to talk with folks like you. You see, he said, I'm blind".

Oh God, forgive me when I whine, I have two eyes, the world is mine.

Later while walking down the street, I saw a child with eyes of blue,

He stopped and watched the others play, he did not know what to do.

I stopped a moment then I said, "Why don't you join the others dear?"

He looked ahead without a word, and then I knew he could not hear.

Oh God, forgive me when I whine, I have two ears, the world is mine.

With feet to take me where I go and eyes to see the sunsets glow.

With ears to hear what I would know.

Oh God, forgive me when I whine, I'm blest indeed, the world is mine.

When I have a particularly bad stretch of fallen transactions, missed listings, or lost buyers, I reread this poem and it reminds me that things are not so bad after all.

Hopefully, the points made in this chapter will help you, the reader, to gain some semblance of the peace and tranquility that make our journey through life so much more purposeful and less stressful.

Peace of mind is important to well-being, to successful achievement and happiness. How is it attained? One of the most meaningful passages in the bible says, "Thou wilt keep him in perfect peace, whose mind is stayed on thee." Isaiah 26:3.

If we trust in the Lord, have faith in Him and realize that He loves us with an all-consuming love, then no matter how often we fall by the wayside, our journey through life will be less stressful and less fearful and less fraught with worry. We will then experience the joy that He wants us to have throughout our life.

Stress

I guess you could say I have been the walking poster child of a stress-filled, high-powered Realtor! I love what I do and enjoy the thrill of putting a deal together.

In my chapter on Energy Management, I mentioned how misuse of energy management principles contributed to my heart going out of rhythm. I want to mention it briefly here again as well, since it ties in with my points on stress.

It was some time in 1985 and my wife, Mary Jean, and I were going to 5:30 p.m. Catholic mass at Saint Louis Church in Englewood, Colorado. As happened all too often I was running to get to church before mass started.

I started to feel light-headed and a bit dizzy but managed to get through the mass. I was not feeling well at all, and Mary Jean suggested (actually demanded) that we get me checked out at Swedish Hospital, which was only a few blocks away. I found myself in a hospital bed hooked up to a monitor. The verdict: my heart was out of rhythm and I needed to be cardioverted [shocked] back into rhythm.

Wow! Was I scared! I had always been able to handle my stress and in fact enjoyed always operating full bore. But I was pulled up short! I began to realize that my fast-paced life was catching up with me. So what to do about it?

Through a series of contacts I was introduced to Dr. Robert Eliot, a famed cardiologist and internationally known expert on stress-related heart problems. Dr. Eliot suffered his own stress-related heart attack and took stress management out of pop psychology and placed it into mainstream medicine.

He ran his own world-renowned life stress simulation lab and clinic in Phoenix, Arizona, and I immediately set up an appointment to see him at his clinic. In conjunction with my visit I was given a series of tests, including the Self-Evaluation Test, Form 1, Stressful Attitudes Test, and the Self-Evaluation Test, Form II, the Life-Event Test. These tests are found in the Appendix.

My test results told me a lot about myself, much of which was quite troubling to me. I was (and to a certain extent still am) a "hot reactor," where my body overreacts dangerously to such common occurrences as losing a listing or missing a plane flight.

As part of my visit to the clinic, I was given a series of tapes (now they would be called CDs) and a copy of Dr. Eliot's book *Is It Worth Dying For?* I started to do research on stress and found that it was indeed a modern epidemic, as witness the following:

Stress Statistics

- More than five billion doses of tranquilizers were prescribed last year.

- Every year, Americans spend more than $600 million on tranquilizers, barbiturates, and anti-depressants ... and millions more on alcohol.

- More than $400 million is spent each year on antacids.

- An estimated 8 million Americans have ulcers.

- About one of every five men will have a heart attack before age 60.

- At least 25 million Americans have high blood pressure.

- Each year in the United States, 30,000 suicides and millions of cases of coronary artery disease are attributed to occupational and environmental stress.

- The medical profession has found more Americans suffer from stress-related health problems than from the common cold.

Source: Effective Learning Systems

Indeed, the physician, William Harvey, recognized way back in the year 1623 that "every affection of the mind that is attended with either pain or pleasure, hope or fear, is the cause of an agitation whose influence extends to the heart."

Essentially, Dr. Eliot and his staff told me that the majority of their patients' visits were related to unrelieved stress, and that the circuits of those patients were overloaded. They said that controlling unnecessary stress was probably the single most important key to preventing heart attacks, and that very likely stress was the greatest single contributor to illness in the industrialized world.

On page 17 of his book, Dr. Eliot references Peggy Lee's mournful song "Is That All There is?", saying that he found many people going through his clinic were really uncertain about what they really wanted out of life or what they realistically could achieve. Often, they struggled to gain what society values instead of developing their own personal values. Gradually life begins to seem empty, the future hollow. These people, he found, are anxious and angry about losing control of their lives. They often avoid turning their anger outward, for fear of losing even more. Instead, they turn it inward, on the only "safe" target — themselves.

The following is quoted directly from page 18 of Dr. Eliot's hardcover book:

> *"Sufferers from chronic stress pay a high price for losing a sense of control over their lives — they often feel a loss of identity and self-esteem as well. It is in trying to regain this crucial sense of control that many cross the line from productive into self-destructive*

behaviors. The irony is that their feelings of stress result not from chance, but from choice.

It took a heart attack for me [Dr. Eliot speaking] to make some new choices, to get out of the trap of joyless struggle. Now after eighteen years of research on stress and the heart, I am convinced that the question "Is that all there is?" is the best clue to the cause of harmful, long-term stress: the sense of being trapped, hopeless, and helpless to get what you really want out of life.

How about you? Check yourself out with this simple question. Don't stop and think about it. Answer immediately with your first gut response:

Are you winning?

If you answered "Yes," without thinking about what you "ought" to say, chances are you feel you can rise to the challenges in your life and look forward to new ones. "Winning" in this sense means feeling able to learn from your mistakes, being open to new options, and having a sense of control over your life.

If you answered "No," chances are that you see yourself in a losing situation, without enough control over your life. You are a high-stress risk."

As mentioned earlier, I learned from my experiences at Dr. Eliot's clinic that I tend to be a "hot reactor" in that I have to work hard to manage the anger and anxiety that I feel in stressful situations. As a "hot reactor," I tend to overreact to stress with extreme blood pressure and chemical changes. However, through what I learned at the clinic, I know that it is important for me not to take things so seriously, and to get them in perspective. Each day I simply say the self-talk "I like myself," and I say it over and over, day after day – when no one is around; this really helps relieve my stress!

One of the most helpful analogies from my experience at the clinic was Dr. Eliot asking me, "What is the most stressful experience you can imagine right now?" I told him probably to drive up to my home in the evening and see my next door neighbor's home with my biggest competitor's "For Sale" sign on that neighbor's lawn! This is a neighbor I have known for 25 years; our kids have grown up together, and we are best friends. Then, Dr. Eliot asked me, "Ok, Jim, for this listing not to have taken place with your competitor, but for you to have the listing, what would you give up in return? Would you have your right leg cut off?" "No!" "How about your left hand index finger?" "No!" "Well, what would you give up?" I answered, "well, maybe a good healthy scratch on my right thumb!"

Then Dr. Eliot gave me the clincher – he said, "Jim, here is the point: when you saw that competitor's sign on your next door neighbor's lawn, your stress level went up to the same degree as if your leg had indeed been cut off. That is totally unhealthy, and the stress level is totally disproportionate to the event that caused your stress level to shoot up at a level so dangerous to your body."

This is an analogy that I have never forgotten after all these years and it reminds me to keep things in perspective – it is not worth dying for!

I want to note that for a period of a year or two I also met with the late Dr. Tom Budzynski of Denver for meditation and relaxation training. I would meet him in his office here in Denver, and he would check my blood pressure and my relaxation ability as I listened to his calming recordings. That training was very helpful to me as well, and to this day the techniques that I learned from Dr. Budzynski help me when I get stressed.

Obviously during the day the stress level can really build up for me. One of the best stress relievers I have found was given to me by the health and nutrition expert, Dr. Andrew Weil. He says that as we increase our stress level during the day, we tend to breathe more shallowly and our oxygen levels decrease. To correct this condition and to relieve our stress, Dr. Weil says to do the following: breathe in deeply through your nose (not through your mouth), as you count to four, while at the same time pushing your stomach out as you do so rather than sucking it in; while continuing to hold your breath as you counted to four, count to seven; then let your breath out as you simultaneously count to eight. Do this exercise three to four times in a row, and your stress level will go way down. In fact, as the stress leaves my body my eyes actually water! I really recommend this stress-relieving exercise, as well as the practice of yoga, which also emphasizes the importance of deep, proper breathing techniques.

I have learned to manage my time and to sit down and plan my day so I have some semblance of control over it, and go over the list of the things I want and need to accomplish. Things do not have to be perfect. Perfectionism is self-destructive because I have made the game impossible to win. Dr. Eliot says to remove the words "should" and "have to" from our vocabulary. He further says that what I do does not determine my value as a person. Genuine feelings of self-worth come from inside me, not from others' responses to what I do. This helps to let go of the fear of failure. Giving up perfectionism does not mean giving up doing a good job, but rather letting go of believing that it's got to be perfect every time for me to feel acceptable and adequate. Even machines need down time, and how much more important is it for us to take time to refuel our body and to regain our enthusiasm?

I have further learned to cool my "hot reactor" tendencies by doing constructive self-talks, to exercise and to realize that I have the luxury at this stage of my career to not have to work with clients that really stress me out; I can choose my clients. I no longer drive myself to achievement at all costs, ignoring the cries of my body. I have learned the value of the lifesaving word "no." As mentioned in an earlier chapter, my wife and I take brisk walks almost every day, and that is our time to get caught up. During that walk, we pray by name for those who have passed away, and then for those that are ill. In the evening before retiring I do some meditative reading to calm my spirit. Very importantly, work is not the frantic experience it once was; it is not the deadly serious and exclusive source of my self-esteem. As has been said, I don't sweat the small stuff – and it's all small stuff. Thanks to Dr. Eliot,

I have learned that most of the time you can't fight, and you can't flee, but you can learn to flow. I have further learned increasingly not to let other people's opinion of me matter so much. As an old sage once mentioned, "To thine own self be true, and all good things will flow to you." Also, the ancient Greeks said, "Nothing in excess." In the final analysis, love, family, and other relationships are all-important, with the overall goal to love your neighbor as yourself.

Finally, the syndicated columnist, Harvey Mackay, who is quoted in various chapters throughout this book, shares some thoughts and wisdom with us in his column entitled "Recognizing, relieving stress is important for your health," as it appeared in the March 8, 2008 issue of the now-defunct Denver *Rocky Mountain News*.

In that article he says that when you feel the frustration levels going up, it might be time to take a break or go for a brisk walk and focus on something that makes you happy. He says you should try to remember you don't have to accomplish everything in one day.

As he goes on to say, we need some stress relief often during the day. We seem to be hurrying someplace important most of the time. The Center for Spirituality and Healing at the University of Minnesota offers these 10 stress-busting tips:

1. Be completely present for whatever you are doing.
2. Include something you consider beautiful in your life on a daily basis. For example, fresh flowers.

3. As often as possible, participate in activities you enjoy.

4. Keep your pace relaxed – that includes walking, working, and eating.

5. Take a break after meals to relax.

6. If possible, go outside once a day and enjoy the simple things in life, like the scenery, the weather, and the laughter of children playing.

7. Take notice of the tension in your body during the day. Breathe deeply and gently stretch any area that feels tense.

8. When you catch your mind racing and worrying, breathe deeply and gently shift your focus to something in the moment.

9. Wear comfortable, loose clothing whenever possible.

10. Don't hold your feelings in day after day. Find a safe place where you can express and embrace them.

Dealing with our stress is central to our well-being, both on the job and after hours. Mackay also says it is important to recognize the signs of an unhealthy level of stress. In *The 10-Minute Guide to Stress Management* (Macmillan 2000), author Jeff Davidson identifies some of the symptoms of unhealthy stress levels: anger; irritability; anxiety; depression; headaches; high blood pressure; sweaty palms; rapid heartbeat; dizziness; cold hands and feet; shortness of breath, and chest pain.

Over the years, Mackay has collected a small library of light-hearted but wise words dealing with stress management, and here are some of his favorites:

- Accept that some days you're a pigeon, and some days you're a statue.

- Always keep your words soft and sweet, just in case you have to eat them.

- If you lend someone $100 and never see that person again, it was probably worth it.

- No one cares if you can't dance well. Just get up and dance.

- If everything's coming your way, you're in the wrong lane.

- Don't cry because it's over. Smile because it happened.

- A truly happy person is one who can enjoy the scenery along the detour.

- Stress often gives a little thing a big shadow.

Stress has been my own worst enemy over the years, but I have been bound and determined not to let it rule me; it has been a difficult process, but I have learned how to control the stress in my life! Hopefully, the points made in this chapter will be helpful as well to you, the reader.

6.

Happiness and Gratitude, Perseverance and Persistence

Happiness and Gratitude

To many people, "gratitude" and "happiness" smack of being the consummate of platitudes, as it could easily be said that everyone wants to be happy, and to be grateful for that happiness. But, as I noted in my comments in the chapter on "Fear and Worry," many of us spend much of our lives not being happy, and in fact we all too often spend a good portion of our time on earth being miserable. So, it does behoove us to look at what constitutes happiness and what we can do to increase its presence in our lives.

I am somewhat ashamed to say that while the purpose of life is to find happiness, for a good portion of my sales career I had not been truly happy. Why is that? Well, as mentioned in my comments in the chapter on "Comparison - Helpful or Harmful," our modern, competitive culture makes it very hard for us to be happy and grateful. These two attributes are indeed intertwined but, as Brother David Steindl-Rast, a Catholic Benedictine monk and scholar says, "It is not happiness that makes us grateful. It is gratefulness that makes us happy. Every moment is a gift." There is no certainty that we will have another moment, with all the opportunity that it contains.

It has taken me a long time, but I have more and more found in my sales career that gratitude means moving from counting my burdens to counting my blessings. I have a gratitude journal and every night I enter into that journal what I have been grateful for that day. Doing this keeps me centered and reminds me that life for the most part is really a lot better than it sometime seems. Gratitude allows me to see what is good and right in the world, and not just what is bad and wrong. As Brother Steindl-Rast further explains, "A grateful world is a world of joyful people. Grateful people are joyful people. A grateful world is a happy world." It is not joy that makes us grateful; it is gratitude that makes us joyful.

In the wonderful book entitled *The Book of Joy*, where His Holiness the Dalai Lama and Archbishop Desmond Tutu are interviewed during the course of a week together, they reference University of California, Davis Professor Robert Emmons, who tells us the positive findings that grateful people do not seem to ignore or deny the negative aspects of life; they simply choose to appreciate what is positive as well. To expand upon this point, throughout each day we have the tremendous power to choose. As one person put it, each day we can:

Chose to love ... rather than hate.

Choose to laugh ... rather than cry.

Choose to create ... rather than destroy.

Choose to persevere ... rather than quit.

Choose to praise ... rather than gossip.

Choose to heal ... rather than wound.

Choose to give ... rather than steal.

Choose to act ... rather than procrastinate.

Choose to grow ... rather than rot.

Choose to pray ... rather than curse.

Choose to live ... rather than die.

Further, all of us have a choice of whether to be takers or givers. As the great football player and coach, Tony Dungy, says in a reading from his book, *The One-Year Uncommon Life*, "Takers are concerned more with receiving value from others' lives than adding value to them. But giving is more rewarding and actually adds to our lives as well. We should value all that we have – treasures, gifts, abilities, family, and friends, as being God's and that are on loan to us. In all of our daily activities we have a choice of when to give or to take; in the long run giving makes us happier. The Lord himself says 'I will not be outdone in my generosity.'"

As professor Emmons states, "People with a strong disposition toward gratitude have the capacity to be empathetic and to take the perspective of others. They are rated as more generous and more helpful by people in their social networks." The Dalai Lama and the Archbishop point out that people with this disposition are more likely to have helped someone with a personal problem or to have offered emotional support to others. They found that people who were grateful possessed more positive emotions, a more positive attitude, were more satisfied with life and had lower levels of stress and depression.

The Book of Joy further speaks to the fact that gratitude naturally leads to a tendency to be kind and generous toward others which then leads to compassion and generosity. Basically, when we fully recognize all that we have been given, it is natural for us to want to care for and give to others. "A compassionate concern for the well-being of others is that source of happiness," says the Dalai Lama. It is the message of love, of compassion; the word "compassion" literally means "suffering with." Very significantly, he says that "there is more to life than increasing its speed."

I have been learning the importance of compassion as a means of attaining happiness but it has been hard for me. I have always felt that sales is so competitive and it is such a "dog-eat-dog" profession, that I was always fundamentally competing against everyone and everything. I tended to think of compassion as a luxury and something to focus on briefly as I was trying to lay the groundwork for another sale. Due to stress, I have had episodes of dizziness and have found that I need to watch my blood pressure. I find that when I am more compassionate, kind, and empathetic, these stress issues reduce significantly.

When I am truly focused on wanting what is best for the other person, life is better for me and I am happier. I have also learned that self-compassion, virtually the same as self-acceptance, is very important, and as I mentioned earlier, it is actually important for me to have compassion for my frailties and faults, recognizing that I am vulnerable and limited like all people. I have found that the more I accept myself with my vulnerability and humanity, the more I can accept the humanity of others. This has been hard for me to accept but as I mentioned earlier, I am learning that "beyond a reasonable discipline (I need to) be good to myself."

In the final analysis I have learned that I am most joyful when I focus on others, not on myself, and that really bringing joy to others is the fastest way to experience joy myself. So being generous (being charitable) results in a deepening relationship with others. Joy is not something to learn but rather it is something to live, and as *The Book of Joy* states in its last sentence, "Our greatest joy is lived in deep, loving and generous relationships with others." Philippians 4:4 says it well, "Always be full of joy in the Lord. I say it again – rejoice." Thessalonians 5:16-18 adds the following: "Always be joyful. Never stop praying. Be thankful in all circumstances for this is God's will for you who belong in Christ Jesus." So our God tells us that we are not just occasionally to rejoice, but always to be living "full of joy."

These verses naturally lead to a discussion of the importance of attitude, covered earlier. In *Man's Search for Meaning*, Viktor Frankl mentions the unspeakable horrors of his long imprisonment in the Nazi concentration camps of Dachau and Auschwitz; his father, mother, brother and wife had died in similar camps, yet despite losing all his possessions, always being hungry and cold, and expecting his own execution to come at any moment, he still found that life was worth living. His captors had not been able to take away "the ability to choose [his] attitude despite [his] given set of circumstances." His experiences remind all of us that we can't always choose our circumstances, but we can always choose our attitude, i.e., how we react to those circumstances. We can choose to be joyful, happy, and compassionate, or be mad, unhappy, and not compassionate. The choice is ours.

In writing this chapter I found that happiness, gratitude, compassion, kindness, and the like, are so closely intertwined as to be a real challenge to discuss them separately; in fact, I have found it is almost impossible to separate them.

I think it is important not to think of these virtues only at Thanksgiving each year, but to practice them all year. Those in the know say we should start with interior gratitude, the practice of giving thanks privately. Next, they say, move on to exterior gratitude, which focuses on public expression. Martin Seligman, father of the field of study known as positive psychology, gives some practical suggestions on how to do this. In his best-selling book, *Authentic Happiness*, he recommends that we express gratitude in letters and e-mails to loved ones and colleagues. He suggests making it as routine as morning coffee. For example, write two short e-mails each morning to family, friends, or colleagues, thanking them for who they are and for what they do.

In my own real estate team of four, we have promised each other that among the four of us, we will make an honest effort to send out 25 hand-written appreciation/thank you notes each week. We place a nice commemorative stamp on the envelope (not a metered stamp). We get so many e-mails each day, but I have found that when I receive a hand-written note, I open it because it is so unusual to receive one! Sending these notes just makes me feel good, and I believe the practice separates me and my team from the real estate sales pack, so to speak. I find myself looking for people to whom I can show honest, sincere appreciation, and my team and I are excited to send them the note.

It is also important to be grateful for the small, unapparent things that we experience as we go through life. These in many ways are as important as the more obvious parts of life, like a happy marriage, healthy kids, living in America, and the like. On a recent trip to China, I was struck by the lack of the basics of a toilet and running water, something we just take for granted here in the United States.

The great philosopher, Cicero, many years ago said that gratitude is not only the greatest of virtues, but the parent of all the others. Melody Beattie says, "Gratitude unlocks the fullness of life. It turns what we have into enough and more. It turns denial into acceptance, chaos to order, and confusion to clarity. It can turn a meal into a feast, a house into a home, a stranger into a friend." Desiderius

Erasmus is quoted as saying that "the summit of happiness is reached when a person is ready to be what he is." Maya Angelou puts it well when she says, "I've learned that people will forget what you said, people will forget what you did, but people will never forget how you made them feel."

Being an English major in college, I have always been interested in the root origin of words and have found that the word "gratitude" is derived from the Latin "gratia" meaning "favor," and "gratus," meaning "pleasing." All derivatives from this Latin root have to do with kindness, generousness, gifts, the beauty of giving and receiving, and the like. Gratitude is pleasing and feels good. Gratitude is also motivating in that when we feel grateful, we are moved to share the goodness we have received with others.

Gratitude matters because if every grateful action were suddenly eliminated, society (at least as we know it) would break apart. Gratitude is the key to happiness, and experts say that consistently being a happy person can add as much as nine years to our life expectancy!

G.K. Chesterton says that gratitude produces the most purely joyful moments that have been known to man.

Previously I have stated the importance of getting adequate sleep, and it is important enough that I am again addressing it here. Sleep disturbance and poor sleep quality have been identified as central indicators of poor overall well-being. People whose sleep is routinely disrupted have high levels of stress hormones and compromised immune function. Should these patterns persist, down the road the sleep-deprived persons face an increased risk of physical disease and premature mortality. Why is this? Sleep is a restorative process that serves to repair, maintain, and enhance our body's physiological capacities. Without such restoration, the wear and tear on our bodies' systems threatens our long-term health and even our survival. It may sound simplistic, but the evidence cannot be ignored: if we want to sleep more soundly, count blessings, not sheep.

The more grateful a person is the less depressed they are. Why? Because that person feels esteemed and validated. However, consumerism fuels ingratitude. Advertisers purposely invoke feelings of comparison and ingratitude by leading us to perceive that our lives are incomplete unless we buy what they are selling. Here is a frightening statistic: by the age of 21, the average adult will have seen 1 million TV commercials!

Prayers of gratitude are the most powerful form of prayer. Religious writings provide some pointed examples of ingratitude. In some spiritual traditions, ingratitude toward God is considered the worst sin and the source of all human misery. Saint Ignatius of Loyola wrote:

"In the light of the Divine Goodness, it seems to me that ingratitude is the most abominable of sins and that it should be detested in the sight of our Creator and Lord by all of His creatures who are capable of enjoying His divine and everlasting glory. It is a forgetting of the graces, benefits, and blessings received, and as such it is the cause, beginning, and origin of all sins and misfortunes."

The benefits of living a life of gratitude are many. Some of those are:

1. Improves your attitude: expressing gratitude makes you feel more positive and optimistic, and this can reduce stress and help in the improvement of your overall mental fortitude.

2. Builds stronger relationships. A simple "thank you" lays the groundwork for a stronger relationship, whether you are dealing with a loved one or a stranger. When you say "thanks," you are acknowledging a person for their help, and that acknowledgement can encourage them to feel special.

3. Improves your mental health. When you feel upset or frustrated, write down what you are thankful for. Studies show that by expressing gratitude you are better able to deal with your emotions, and it may even help reduce depression.

4. Enhances your physical health. Studies show a strong correlation between gratitude and good health. People who are thankful tend to be healthier.

5. Boosts your self -esteem by helping you maintain perspective and be less likely to compare yourself to other people.

6. As mentioned, you sleep better.

7. Increases your empathy for others. Grateful people are less likely to retaliate when experiencing negativity from others.

8. Spreads happiness!

9. Become more resilient!

Conversely, it is equally important to recognize and deal with the roadblocks to happiness, as stated by Peter McWilliams, co-author of *Do it! Let's Get Off Our BUTS!* Peter says the first roadblock is **FEAR;** however, the good news is fear provides the energy to do your best in a new situation. The second is **GUILT**, i.e., anger at ourselves. We did something we didn't think we should have done and therefore we feel bad about it. Third, is **UNWORTHINESS.** You are worthy of anything you want, but you are not able to have everything you want at one time. The solution is to pick the one thing you want most, make yourself worthy of it and don't worry about the rest. Success follows success. Fourth, **DISCOURAGEMENT**. In French, the word "Coeur" means heart. Encouragement is courage, strength from the heart. When we act from the heart, we act with courage. Discouragement takes courage away and overcoming this is simply a matter of taking away the "dis" and substituting "en." Fifth, **BAD AND TROUBLED TIMES.** "Bad" and "Troubled" are both judgments on a situation that can also be called change. Change is inevitable, and we should welcome it for the opportunities that it brings.

Many ways exist to say thanks. Here are some good and concrete examples for doing so.

1. Give food. Find out the person's favorite treat and deliver it in person.

2. As we have said earlier, a heartfelt, handwritten note card saying why you are grateful goes a long way.

3. Return the favor. For example, if a neighbor picked up your newspaper and mail while you were on vacation, offer to do the same in return.

4. Pay it forward. One example that I experienced personally was years ago the person in the car ahead of me on a toll road paying my toll for me when it became my turn at the gate; it blew me away!

5. Deliver flowers or a plant. When I was selling pots and pans to get through college, I had an arrangement with the local florist where he would deliver three tea roses in a vase with my hand-written note the day after I got an accepted sales contract; the cost, believe it or not, was $1.25 delivered! Most of my sales were to younger girls just out of high school and I had the lowest cancellation rate of all my 85 sales colleagues!

6. Give them something useful; get to know the person's interests, e.g., if they are into wine, bring them a nice bottle of wine.

7. Give a gift card. You may not know the person well but know something about their daily life. For example, if they do a lot of driving around town, get them a Starbucks card so they can enjoy a coffee on the go.

8. If you are into social media, brag on them by tagging them in a post thanking them for their help; your comment will be shared with their family, friends, and colleagues.

9. Donate money to a charity in their name.

I have a personal story here. My wife and I adopted our three children. As mentioned in Chapter 1, our first child, Eric, fell into a deep coma when he was 11 months old and passed away when he was 15 years old. As a result, I have always had a soft spot in my heart for life-threatened children and have been on the board of the local Denver Chapter of Make-A-Wish Foundation. Every year at holiday time I send a letter out to my top clients, wishing them holiday blessings and telling them that I am making a donation in their honor to the Make-A-Wish Foundation. I have many clients thanking me for doing this, and it is very fulfilling for me personally to make this donation to a charity that is so meaningful to me.

One of the highlights of my real estate career occurred on November 11, 1976, when I personally received a plaque presented by the famous motivational speaker and writer, the late Og Mandino, that has "The Salesman's Prayer" inscribed on it. Og says the following about happiness, and I think it is worth noting here:

Happiness ... is being satisfied with what I've got and what I haven't got. My needs are few. So long as I have something to do, someone to love, and something to hope for, I shall be happy ... The only source of happiness is within me, and I will begin to share it.

– From *The Choice*, Og Mandino

As the prolific writer Dennis Waitley puts it, "Happiness cannot be traveled to, owned, earned, or worn. It is the spiritual experience of living every minute with love, grace and gratitude."

By the way, the word "kind" can be included with the virtues that I have been referencing in this chapter. A great book has been written by David Lubetzky entitled *Do The Kind Thing*. Lubetzky is the CEO of KIND healthy snacks, and the social mission of his company is to make the world a little *kinder*. His *modus operandi* is to think boundlessly, work purposefully, and live passionately. The book is excellent and I highly recommend it. By definition, "kindness" encompasses taking the feelings of others into consideration, as well as sympathy, empathy, compassion, thoughtfulness, gentleness, and caring.

All in all, in the best and most complete sense of the words we can summarize this entire chapter in the biblical quotes of, "do unto others as you would have them do unto you," and to "love your neighbor as yourself." It is doing the right things at all times and especially if no one is watching!

If we do this, each of us will be the poster child for someone who exudes happiness and gratitude as well as their intricately intertwined companion virtues of joy, compassion, generosity, love, empathy, and kindness.

Perseverance and Persistence

Throughout my real estate sales career I have always prided myself on being persistent and persevering to get the job done. When starting to write this chapter I struggled a bit with the two words "perseverance" and "persistence," and their meanings. I felt they both represented important attributes of a salesperson who excelled, and I was not sure if they had somewhat different meanings. So, I went to the dictionary and found that they basically were synonyms, i.e., they had basically the same meaning. "Persistence" speaks of working hard on a particular challenge, especially in the face of opposition, and synonymous for both of the words are the additional words "doggedness" and "steadfastness." So, for purposes of this chapter, I will treat the words "perseverance" and "persistence" as being synonymous.

Stefan Swanepoel is a nationally recognized real estate businessperson and is the author of at least 20 books and reports. He gives us a good understanding of perseverance when he states that, "Perseverance means to continue steadily in some state, purpose, course of action or the like, in spite of opposition. Perseverance means to never give up. Failure is what happens when you quit, not when you continue. The road to success is dotted with parking lots filled with the failure of those that were not willing to get up and try again."

Winston Churchill said it very tellingly when he emphasized to "never, never, never give up!" Echoing this admonition, the syndicated columnist, Harvey Mackay, referenced several times in this book, says, "There are three things in life that you must always remember: (1) Never give up. (2) Never give up. (3) Never give up. He goes on to say: "Remember the 10 most powerful two-letter words in the English language – if it is to be, it is up to me. In any difficult endeavor, perseverance is the greatest asset anyone can have."

A true story from my sales experience that comes to mind and that stresses the importance of perseverance, of not giving up, occurred several years ago with one of my listings; the story goes like this:

The listing was located in the exclusive Denver Cherry Hills subdivision and it had been listed by me for some time. The seller was very happy with my services but my listing was coming up for renewal, and he told me he was going to make a switch of listing agents just for the sake of making a switch – one of those irrational statements that infuriates all of us Realtors. I was getting almost a showing a day and knew the house would sell momentarily. I also knew that the seller was somewhat strapped financially. So, I did something I had never done before: I told him if he would re-list with me for an additional month, I would pay his house payment for that month in the approximate amount of $2,600.00. If the home sold in that month's period, the seller would reimburse me at closing for that house payment with no interest and of course would owe me my commission. If the home did not sell during that period, the seller owed me nothing and was free to list with another broker. The seller agreed to the 30-day extension, and as it turned out I sold the home on a co-op basis during the 30-day extension period and made a $25,000 commission as well as being reimbursed the $2,600.00 house payment at closing. In retrospect I have found the story to be a good example of perseverance, i.e., of not giving up when the situation looked almost impossible. The following poem, "Don't Quit", author unknown, also speaks to the importance of perseverance.

Don't Quit

When things go wrong, as they sometimes will,

When the road you're trudging seems all uphill,

When the funds are low, and the debts are high,

And you want to smile, but you have to sigh,

When care is pressing you down a bit –

Rest when you must, but don't you quit.

Life is queer with its twists and turns,

As every one of us sometimes learns,

And many a fellow turn about

When he might have won had he stuck it out.

Don't give up though the pace seems slow –

You may succeed with another blow.

Often the goal is nearer than

It seems to a faint and faltering man.

Often the struggler has given up

When he might have captured the victor's cup,

How close he was to the golden crown.

Success is failure turned inside out –

The silver tint of the clouds of doubt,

And you never can tell how close you are,

It may be near when it seems so afar.

So, stick to the fight when you're hardest hit –

It's when things seem worst that you mustn't quit.

It is so important to follow up and not give up on a client. The statistics are very telling. Just think about it for a minute:

- 80 percent of all new sales are made after the fifth call on the same prospect

- 48 percent of salespeople make one call and cross the prospect off
- 35 percent quit after the second call; 12% call only three times
- Only 10 percent keep calling
- The result is 10 percent of the salespeople make 80 percent of the sales!

I have found that salespeople are impatient and often take it personally if they do not get a callback. I think we forget sometimes that the lack of a callback is not meant to be mean or inconsiderate; life happens, and the prospect does not necessarily have top of mind to return our call. We need to keep calling until, in the nicest sense of the word, they either set up an appointment with us or tell us they are no longer interested. The key point to keep in mind is that a refusal is not a personal rejection.

Early in my real estate selling career I would be totally decimated when I would get a door slammed in my face or when I would see a competing Realtor's sign in front of my neighbor's yard. (I have to tell you, these situations somewhat still bother me!) However, I have learned that the people are not rejecting me personally, but as repeated in an earlier chapter, they are rather rejecting my proposition which is to work with them on the purchase or sale of a home. It is critical to not take this rejection personally, but rather to look at each rejection as being a step closer to a positive, as well as being closer to an offer to help the client find or sell a home.

The late Steve Jobs, founder of Apple, put it very well when he said, "I'm convinced that about half of what separates the successful entrepreneurs from the non-successful ones is pure perseverance."

President Calvin Coolidge has been quoted many times with the following:

"Nothing in the world can take the place of persistence. Talent will not; nothing is more common than unsuccessful men with talent. Genius will not; unregarded genius is almost a proverb. Education will not; the world is full of educated derelicts. Persistence and determination alone are omnipotent."

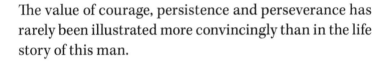

The value of courage, persistence and perseverance has rarely been illustrated more convincingly than in the life story of this man.

	Age
Failed in business	22
Ran for Legislature-defeated	23
Again failed in business	24
Elected to Legislature	25
Sweetheart died	26
Had a nervous breakdown	27
Defeated for Speaker	29
Defeated for Elector	31
Defeated for Congress	34
Elected to Congress	37

Defeated for Congress	39
Defeated for Senate	46
Defeated for Vice President	47
Defeated for Senate	49
Elected President of the United States	51

That's the record of Abraham Lincoln, 16th President of the United States!

It is not easy to fail so often and still keep going, and yet ironically the more one fails, the greater the probability of succeeding. The great basketball player, Michael Jordan, covers this as well as anyone:

> *"I have missed more than 9,000 shots in my career.*
>
> *I have lost almost 300 games.*
>
> *On 26 occasions I have been entrusted to take*
>
> *The game winning shot and missed.*
>
> *I have failed over and over again in my life ...*
>
> *And that is why I succeed."*

As mentioned earlier in this chapter, years ago I was honored to receive an award in person from Og Mandino, who has written one of the all-time classics in sales training and salesmanship entitled *The Greatest Salesman in the World*. In this book, Og presents the 10 basic rules for effective selling, and he does it remarkably well.

His 10th rule is "I will persist until I succeed." My note on the inside of my copy of his book shows that I purchased it on March 23, 1971, and its contents have been an inspiration to me ever since. Here are some of Og's comments on the importance of persistence:

"I will never consider defeat and I will remove from my vocabulary such words and phrases as quit, cannot, unable, impossible, out of the question, improbable, failure, unworkable, hopeless, and retreat; for they are the words of fools. I will avoid despair but if this disease of the mind should infect me then I will work on in despair. I will toil and I will endure. I will ignore the obstacles at my feet and keep mine eyes on the goals above my head, for I know that where dry desert ends, green grass grows.

I will persist until I succeed.

I will remember the ancient law of averages and I will bend it to my good. I will persist with knowledge that each failure to sell will increase my chance for success at the next attempt. Each nay I hear will bring me closer to the sound of yea. Each frown I meet only prepares me for the smile to come. Each misfortune I encounter will carry in it the seed of tomorrow's good luck. I must have the night to appreciate the day. I must fail often to succeed only once.

I will persist until I succeed.

Nor will I allow yesterday's success to lull me into today's complacency, for this is the great foundation of failure. I will forget the happenings of the day that is gone, whether they were good or bad, and greet the new sun with confidence that this will be the best day of my life.

So long as there is breath in me, that long will I persist. For now, I know one of the greatest principles of success; if I persist long enough, I will win.

I will persist.

I will win."

As Thomas A. Edison says so well, our greatest weakness lies in giving up. The most certain way to succeed is always to try just one more time.

Finally, I have always believed with all my heart and soul that if I persist and persevere even when I and everyone else is discouraged, good things happen, and I will succeed, even against all odds. Believe, persist, and win!

7.

SIGNIFICANCE

WHAT IS SIGNIFICANCE? The dictionary defines it as "importance; meaning; the quality of having a meaning." My good friend Brian Buffini says Success is usually measured by comparing ourselves to other people, whereas with Significance we don't compare ourselves with other people but rather we compare ourselves with the gifts that God has given us and our own potential, and how we have used that potential in our own lives.

Mediocrity is established when we focus on our weaknesses. Success and Significance are manifested when we focus on our strengths and create a mechanism to support and improve upon our weaknesses.

The title of my book is **Significance** – *A Lifetime Of Learning, Earning And Love*, and my wife and I, like many of my readers, started from a mode of basic Survival, living from hand to mouth and barely making ends meet. In our case we started married life in a one-bedroom apartment with a king-size bed that we purchased, and a card table and four chairs that we borrowed. When I started in 1970 selling real estate in Aurora, Colorado, my wife and I again lived in a one-bedroom apartment, and I was showing homes in a 1965 Chevrolet with New York license plates; not exactly one's idea of someone that was a pillar of the community! Anyway, we were indeed in Survival mode.

The next step in our journey was the Stability level. Before going any further, I should mention that a key point to all of this discussion is that the different levels must follow each other in sequence. When my wife and I got to the Stability stage level I found that we were in the stage of understanding, where I was learning the real estate business and realizing that I had to be disciplined, set goals, and develop the habits associated with a successful Realtor in order that I would not fall back into Survival mode.

As I moved on to the next level of achievement which Brian calls the Success or the excellence and expectation stage, I found myself refining the goals and habits learned in my Stability stage. I realized that to go from Stability to Success I had to change my thinking; I found this really difficult to do and difficult to keep my thoughts focused and positive. As Proverbs 27:7 says in the bible, "For as a man thinketh in his heart, so is he."

Finally, I personally now have gotten to the final stage of my journey, and that is the Significance stage. In his great book, *Halftime: Moving from Success to Significance*, Bob Buford describes the yearning for Significance, and puts it so well when he says, "One of the most common characteristics of a person who is nearing the end of the first half [of his or her life] is that unquenchable desire to move from Success to Significance. After a first half of building a career and trying to become financially secure, we'd like to do something in the second half that is more meaningful – something that rises above perks and pay checks into the stratosphere of Significance" (page 133).

I have reached a reasonable level of financial independence, our two children are grown and on their own, and I find that most if not all of my personal, financial, and real estate sales goals have been achieved. I now find myself in the mastery stage where I have seemingly mastered my ability to sell and list a home, and am now focusing not on accumulating but on giving back to the real estate industry and to other people in general. I also am able to focus on just being myself rather than having to be someone other than who I am. The old adage of "what you see is what you get" applies here. In this Significance stage, as Brian Buffini so aptly puts it, the philosophy focuses on mentoring and championing others and serving and instructing others. My personal priorities have changed from a competitive and self-centered mode to a mode of focusing on others.

Specifically, in the Significance or mastering stage, my priorities have been changing and I am more aware of the importance of giving back. I am on the board of the Denver Chapter of Make-a-Wish Foundation and The Advisory Board of the University of Colorado School of Business. I derive a lot of satisfaction in being a part of what these boards do for individuals in the Denver community.

My wife and I have worked very hard to be in the position of being able to give back to our children. Even with children who are now adults with their own families, it has been tremendously rewarding for us to continue to be there for them, to support them, and to provide guidance for them. Whether it was helping one get a new business off the ground and subsequently selling it, or providing a place in our basement for the other to stay while transitioning between jobs and cities, we love the continued satisfaction that parenting can provide. And, of course, we are always happy to provide advice in general to our children, if asked.

We have found that family help can even extend to the next generation! We had our grandson, now 24 years old, staying with us for approximately two years while he was taking a 14-month course to become an auto mechanic. During the first four months of schooling we helped him get a 2010 Honda Civic automobile. Shortly thereafter someone backed into him and he learned about filing accident reports and the like. Even though he was not at fault in the accident, he had to be 25 years of age to get a rental car, so my wife and I had to arrange for transportation to and from school for him. The point to all of this is my wife and I modeled for him, hopefully in a meaningful way, with our response to the accident, with our lifestyle, and with the chores we assigned to him to help him earn money for gas and other living expenses.

I have also found myself being asked to go out for breakfast and lunch by some of the younger salespeople in our office who wish to draw upon my 50+ years of selling real estate and hopefully pick up some words of wisdom and advice; I really enjoy being asked to do this, and also enjoy volunteering to do so on my own without being asked. Of course, these in-person get-togethers have unfortunately been curtailed somewhat due to COVID-19.

My three additional real estate team members are doing just fine and the team is functioning well. I am increasingly able to extricate myself from the day-to-day real estate activities and devote more of my time to giving back and to mentoring within the Denver community.

However, I must say that it is still somewhat difficult to just consider up and leaving the real estate business "cold turkey," so to speak. I continue to love what I am doing, and it still is fun and rewarding to negotiate a deal where I can help get the property for less if representing the buyer, or help get more for the property if I am representing the seller. Nevertheless, as my age advances, an increasing number of my real estate contemporaries are either fully retired or close to retirement, and it has made sense for me to at least consider that option.

Also, it still is hard to have a valued past client list with another broker because they believe with me becoming increasingly retired that I am not able to devote my full attention and expertise to their listing. On my part this is just an ego/pride thing and is something that I or anyone moving into real estate retirement needs to deal with.

Another reality that I am very aware of is the disconcerting fact that an ever-increasing number of my colleagues and contemporaries have become ill and are dying, especially with the ravages of the COVID-19 pandemic that has been upon us.

While I am blessed to enjoy good health, I am also realistic and cognizant of the fact that I may not enjoy five, 10, or 15 additional years of that good health or even of life in general. As Dr. Atul Gauwande says in his best-selling book, *Being Mortal*, "Death is normal. Death may be the enemy, but it is also the natural order of things" (page 8). "When the prevailing fantasy is that we can be ageless, the geriatrician's uncomfortable demand is that we accept we are not" (page 46). We need to have the proper perspective on aging, our personal sense of how finite our time in this world is (page 95). "Serious illness or infirmity will strike as inevitable as sunset" (page 23).

As I have grown in the Significance mode and stage of life, I remember a book that I read entitled *The Top Five Regrets of the Dying* by Bronnie Ware. In that book, Bronnie relates her experience as a palliative care nurse and her interviews with several of her patients as they drew closer to passing on.

I recently re-read that book and it has been helpful for me and hopefully for you, the reader, to learn from the regrets of these dying people as they are approaching the end of their lives. They are a constant reminder for me to be so grateful for all my blessings, and also to enjoy each moment of each day.

The first regret is: "I wish I'd had the courage to live a life true to myself, not the life others expected of me." This was the most common of all the five regrets. To live this way requires that we are brave enough to live as we want to, regardless of what other people say or what they think of us. Learning to be kind to oneself and give oneself compassion is all-important here.

The second regret is: "I wish I hadn't worked so hard." Bronnie interviews a man named John, who is dying, and the following quote from him is very telling (pages 77 and 78). "If I can tell you one thing about life, Bronnie, it's this. Don't create a life where you are going to regret working too hard. I can say now that I didn't know I was going to regret it until I was at this time facing the very end. But deep in my heart, I knew I was working too hard. Not just for Margaret [his wife], but for me, too. I would love to have not cared what others thought of me, as I do now. I wonder why we have to wait until we are dying to work things like this out." Shaking his head, he kept talking. "There is nothing wrong with loving your work and wanting to apply yourself to it. But there is so much more to life. Balance is what is important, maintaining balance."

John is talking about his wife, Margaret. He had promised her he would retire in one year after completing just one final deal; sadly, she passed away before that transaction was completed, and their plans for traveling and enjoying the fruits of his achievement were never realized. Especially sad was the fact that he became terminally ill as well.

This regret is especially relevant for me as I have loved my work so much that over the years, I had verged upon being a workaholic.

The third regret is: "I wish I'd had the courage to express my feelings." Here Bronnie interviews Jozsef, and on page 105, he mentions that his regrets were partly for his family, who had seen so little of him for most of their life in Australia. But it was mostly because he felt he had never given them a chance to know him. "I was too scared to let my feelings show. So I worked and worked and kept the family at a distance. They didn't deserve to be so alone. Now I wish they really knew me." He also felt he had missed the opportunity to create loving warmth with his children.

The fourth regret is: "I wish I had stayed in touch with my friends." Bronnie quotes (page 139) from one of her dying patients: "It wasn't just Sundays, though. Loneliness leaves emptiness in the heart that can physically kill you. The ache is unbearable, and the longer it hangs around, the more despair adds to it. Miles of city streets, country roads, and everything in between were walked during those years. Loneliness isn't a lack of people. It is a lack of understanding and acceptance. Huge amounts of people the world over have experienced loneliness in crowded rooms. In fact, being alone in crowded rooms often highlights and exacerbates loneliness."

"It doesn't matter how many people are around you. If there is no one available who understands you, or accepts you as who you are, loneliness can very readily present its agonizing self. It is very different than being alone, as I had loved this often in the past. Being alone can mean you are lonely, *or* you are happy. Loneliness is a longing for the company of one who understands you. Sometimes being alone and loneliness are related, but very often they are not."

Further, Ware quotes another dying person, Elizabeth (page 155), who laments, "Don't lose touch with the friends you value most, Bronnie. Those who accept you as who you are, and who know you very well, are worth more than anything in the end. Don't let life get in the way. Just always know where to find them and let them know you appreciate them in the meantime. Don't be afraid to be vulnerable either. I wasted some time in not being able to let them know what a mess I was."

The fifth and last regret is: "I wish I had let myself be happier." Here Bronnie quotes from Rosemary: "As I came back into her room early one evening, she declared, 'I wish I'd let myself be happier. What a miserable person I have been. I just didn't think I deserved to be. But I do. I know that now. Laughing with you this morning I realized that there was no need at all to feel guilty for being happy.' Sitting down on the side of her bed, I listened as she went on. 'It really is our own choice, isn't it? We can stop ourselves from being happy because we think we don't deserve it, or because we allow the opinions of others to become a part of who we are. But it is not who we are, is it? We can be whoever we allow ourselves to be. My God, why didn't I work this out sooner? What a waste!'"

Lovingly, I smiled at her. "Well, I've been in that place, too, Rosemary. But being gentle and compassionate is a healthier way to treat yourself. At any rate, you've worked it out now, by allowing at least some happiness into your life recently. We've had some beautiful times." Recalling things we had laughed at, Rosemary agreed, and found herself in a happy mood again."

Ware goes on to elaborate further on this (pages 227, 229, 233 and 235):

"It is a pity that being who you truly are requires so much courage. But it does. It takes *enormous* courage at times. Being who you are, whoever that is, sometimes cannot even be articulated at first, not even to yourself. All you know is there is a yearning within that is not being fulfilled by the life you are currently living... Yes, having the courage to be yourself and not who others expect you to be may take a lot of strength and honesty. But so does lying on your deathbed and admitting that you wish you had done it differently... In the end, what matters to people is *how much happiness they have brought to those they love and how much time they spent doing things they themselves loved...* Every single one of us has reasons to feel sorry for ourselves. Every one of us has suffered. But life doesn't owe us anything. We only owe ourselves, to make the most of the life we are living, of the time we have left, and to live in gratitude... Life is over so quickly. It is possible to reach the end with no regrets. It takes some bravery to live it right, to honor the life you are here to live but the choice is yours. So will be the rewards. Appreciate the time you have left by valuing *all* the gifts in your life, and that especially includes your own, amazing self."

A short verse that I ran across recently summarizes much of this very succinctly. I quoted it in an earlier chapter as well. It goes like this: "Whatever you'll wish on your dying day that you had done while healthy – do it now while you still may."

Life is too short to wake up with regrets. So, we should love the people who treat us right and forget about the ones who don't. We should believe everything happens for a reason. If we get a second chance, we should grab it with both hands. If it changes our life, let it. Nobody said life would be easy, they just promised it would be worth it.

Also, friends are like balloons; once we let them go, we might not get them back. Sometimes we get so busy with our own lives and problems that we may not even notice that we've let them fly away. Sometimes we are so caught up in who's right and who's wrong that we forget what's right and wrong. Often we just don't realize what real friendship means until it is too late.

The reason I mention so completely and extensively the five regrets listed above and have devoted so much space to them, is that they are so full of wisdom and we can learn so much from these dying people what they would have done differently. We can and should learn from them before it is too late and apply those lessons to our own life, especially as we move into the level of Significance.

With all of the above being said, one could get a little bit depressed or maybe at least somewhat concerned about the prospect of growing older. At least I had a twinge of that emotion as I was writing this chapter. However, we enjoy a lot of offsetting positives. For example, there is arguably no better time in history to be older and in the Significance mode. Those living in the days of the Roman

Empire had an average life expectancy of a mere 28 years, while today our average life span in much of the world is climbing past 80 years.

Additionally, almost every time we open the newspaper or magazine we learn about some amazing feat or accomplishment being chalked up by people considered "old" by most standards. One's age does not by any means dictate one's ability to accomplish. Reaching that magical retirement age does not mean that one is finished contributing to society. Here are just a few examples of people who refused to "act their age:"

Admiral Rickover, the designer of the first nuclear submarine, was still a consultant to the Navy at the age of 82.

Both **Grandma Moses** and **Georgia O'Keeffe**, American artists, continued to paint well past 90 and into their 100+ years.

Russian artist **Marc Chagall** was designing stained glass windows for churches in many parts of the world at age 90.

Frank Lloyd Wright, considered one of the greatest modern American architects, created an entirely original concept of architecture when he was past 90. Wright was fond of saying, "Youth is quality, and if you have it, you never lose it."

George Bernard Shaw, the Irish dramatist, was still working on a play at 93 when his prolific life ended prematurely due to complications from a broken leg.

Verdi continued to compose operas, as well as the well-known "Requiem." When he was in his 80s, he created a retirement home for musicians.

Arthur Rubinstein gave a concert at Carnegie Hall at age 90. He was almost blind and unable to read the notes. Nevertheless, he played with his usual perfection. Afterwards, he was heard to remark, "The music is in my mind."

Albert Schweitzer was an outstanding German organist and philosopher who created a new life in Africa for the underprivileged. He was a physician, a clergyman, and an expert in music. He was active until age 90.

Pablo Picasso, having painted over 20,000 pictures, is considered by many to be the greatest artist of the 20th century. At 90 he remarked, "I often feel young, like 20, and I am only concerned when I feel that I am aging."

Robert Frost, nearly 87, read his poem, "The Gift Outright," at the inauguration of President John F. Kennedy in 1961.

Historian **Arnold Toynbee** shared this reflection of life at age 81: "As one grows older, the temptation to dwell on the past and to avert one's eyes from the future grows. If one were to fall into this backward-looking stance, one would be as good as dead before physical death had overtaken us. Our minds, so long as they keep their cutting edge, are not bound by our physical limits; they can range over time and space into infinity. To be human is to be capable of transcending oneself."

In summary, each of the "S" stages of life – Survival, Stability, Success and Significance – has their proper order of appearing to us on our life path; they each have their own characteristics and challenges.

Unfortunately, too many people on their life's journey through the four stages become impatient, wanting to skip over one or several of these stages, e.g., skipping from Survival directly to Success while by-passing Stability. This can result in chaos, instability, back-sliding, and loss of momentum.

To get to the Success and Significance stages more quickly, we need to accept the stage that we are currently in, work within it with the goals appropriate to that stage, and keep a positive mental attitude, not trying to short-cut the process.

I am very happy and blessed to now be in the Significance stage of my life. My wife and I, and our entire family for that matter, are healthy, able to travel and enjoy each other's company, and we respect each other for our similarities and differences.

My financial status is such that I am increasingly able to extricate myself from the day-to-day activities of my real estate sales while keeping somewhat active. I enjoy mentoring my great Kentwood Real Estate Team and others, trying to "make a difference" in as many lives as possible.

In the Significance stage, I am no longer tempted to be someone other than who I am and no longer feel obligated to chase perfection in order to be liked. I do not need to wear a mask each day, so to speak. I try to be authentic and, as Brené Brown, quoted previously says, be vulnerable. Also, I try hard to show some grace and cut some slack to those I meet each day.

Life is good, and my wife and I never take a day for granted. We appreciate being given another day to enjoy free from pain. As my wife says, just live in the present and every day is a "present." We thank God every day for the blessings that He has bestowed upon us. It is a real honor and privilege to have reached the Significance stage of our lives, a stage that allows us the opportunity to give back to others in gratitude for the talents and unique gifts that we have been given by our all-loving God and Creator.

My sincere wish is for all of you, my real estate friends and colleagues, to enjoy your own journey as much as I have enjoyed mine, as you move through your life stages of Survival, Stability, and Success, on your way to your own level of Significance, secure in the realization that you are striving as best you can to live a life that truly matters.

APPENDIX

Jim NUSSBAUM CRS, GRI

Personal Service That Will Make You Feel Right At Home

BROKER / PARTNER

TODAY'S DOLLAR-PRODUCTIVE ACTIVITIES

TODAY'S DATE _____

Always *LIST* and *DO* The *MOST* Dollar-Productive Activity First!!

TODAY'S TOP DOLLAR-PRODUCTIVE ACTIVITIES	$ TO BE REALIZED	HR(S) SPENT	$ EARNED / HOUR	NOTES AND FOLLOWUP
☐ 1.	$		$	
☐ 2.	$		$	
☐ 3.	$		$	
☐ 4.	$		$	
☐ 5.	$		$	
☐ 6.	$		$	
☐ 7.	$		$	
☐ 8.	$		$	
☐ 9.	$		$	
☐ 10.	$		$	
TOTALS	$		$	

Call Jim Nussbaum For All Your Denver Area Referrals!!!

Final thought at the end of the day: Have you given and/or received a *"10"* today??

5690 D.T.C. Boulevard, Englewood, CO 80111
Office Toll Free 1-800-723-7653 • Office (303) 773-3399 • Home (303) 794-2050 • FAX (303) 773-1203

The Kentwood Moore Company

DEAR DAD.
I love YOU, BUT
WEN YOUR GON
IT'S NOT THE
same I PLAY WITE
TOYS
BUT WITH OWT
YOU IM SAD
LOVE Katie

Dad-
If you get some spare time or get a day off, these are the things that I'd enjoy doing one on one.
Thank, Katie

☐ Go 2 Circus!
☐ Go Horseback-riding

☐ Play Tennis

☐ Go to a B-Ball game

☐ Go to a Movie

☐ Go Putt-putt golfing

☐ Go Golfing (normal)

☐ Play B-ball, 1 on 1 (at home)

☐ Go to Greenwood together

☐ Play Rackit Ball at club

☐ Go bike riding

SELF EVALUATION TEST
FORM I
STRESSFUL ATTITUDES TEST

	How Often Feeling Occurs (Circle the number under the answer that most applies to you)			
	Almost never	Occasionally	Frequently	Almost always
1. I must not fail.	1	2	3	4
2. Things must be perfect.	1	2	3	4
3. I must do it myself.	1	2	3	4
4. I feel under pressure to succeed all the time.	1	2	3	4
5. I avoid speaking my mind.	1	2	3	4
6. When overworked, I cannot say "no" to new demands without feeling guilty.	1	2	3	4
7. I feel that people should listen better.	1	2	3	4
8. I feel more isolated from my family or close friends.	1	2	3	4
9. My life is running me.	1	2	3	4
10. I feel increasingly cynical and disenchanted.	1	2	3	4
11. Sex seems like more trouble than it's worth.	1	2	3	4
12. I can't seem to get out of bed.	1	2	3	4
13. I feel unrested.	1	2	3	4
14. I'm not where I want to be in my life.	1	2	3	4
15. I consider myself exploited.	1	2	3	4

Subtotal ____ _____ _____ ____

TOTAL _____

15– Low Stress, 16–29 Mild Stress, 30–39 Moderate Stress, 40–60 High Stress

SELF EVALUATION TEST
FORM II
THE LIFE-EVENT TEST

Enter Points	Life Event	Points
_____	Death of spouse	100
_____	Divorce	73
_____	Marital separation	65
_____	Jail term	63
_____	Death of close family member	63
_____	Personal injury or illness	53
_____	Marriage	50
_____	Fired at work	47
_____	Marital reconciliation	45
_____	Retirement	45
_____	Change in family member's health	44
_____	Pregnancy	40
_____	Sex difficulties	39
_____	Addition to family	39
_____	Business readjustment	39
_____	Change in financial state	38
_____	Death of close friend	37
_____	Change to different line of work	36
_____	Change in number of marital arguments	35
_____	Mortgage or loan for major purchase (home, etc.)	31
_____	Foreclosure of mortgage or loan	30
_____	Change in work responsibility	29
_____	Son or daughter leaving home	29
_____	Trouble with in-laws	29
_____	Outstanding personal achievement	28
_____	Spouse begins or stops work	26
_____	Starting or finishing school	26
_____	Change in living conditions	25
_____	Revision of personal habits	24
_____	Trouble with boss	23
_____	Change in work hours, conditions	20
_____	Change in residence	20
_____	Change in school	20
_____	Change in recreational habits	19
_____	Change in church activities	19
_____	Change in social activities	18
_____	Mortgage or loan for lesser purchase (car, TV, etc.)	17
_____	Change in sleeping habits	16
_____	Change in number of family gatherings	15
_____	Change in eating habits	15
_____	Vacation	13
_____	Christmas season	12
_____	Minor violation of the law	11

TOTAL SCORE _____

Reprinted with permission from the *Journal of Psychosomatic Research*, vol. 11, Thomas H. Holmes and Richard R. Rahe, "The Social Readjustment Rating Scale," c) 1967, Pergamon Press, Ltd.

If your score is 300 or more, statistically you stand an almost 80 percent chance of getting sick in the near future. If your score is 150 to 299, the chances are about 50 percent. At less than 150, about 30 percent.

ABOUT THE AUTHOR

Jim Nussbaum was born and raised in Appleton, Wisconsin — the oldest of five siblings who all grew up in a very small, three-bedroom, two-story home. His father worked in a paper mill and when he could not make ends meet, he began working as a straight-commission, door-to-door vacuum cleaner salesman—a job he often struggled with. Watching how his mom, Lucy, and his dad, Len, worked together to get through those tough financial times inspired Jim to develop a work ethic and marriage that have been second to none. He was the first person in his family to attend college—at Saint John's University in Collegeville, Minnesota— where he majored in English and studied the classics. After earning his Master's Degree in Business Administration/Marketing (MBA) from the University of Wisconsin in Madison, Wisconsin, Jim tried a number of career paths before he found his life's true passion: selling residential real estate. He earned his real estate license in 1970 and in 1981 founded The Kentwood Company in Denver, Colorado, along with four other colleagues. Since selling the company in 2007, Jim has continued in a non-ownership capacity to sell residential real estate in Denver with his three teammates. He has had over 2,800 closings in his career and over $1.3 billion in sales. Besides selling homes, Jim loves to read, travel, and enjoy great food. He is married to Mary Jean, his wife of 54 years, and loves spending time with his children, Dan and Kate, and their families.

CPSIA information can be obtained
at www.ICGtesting.com
Printed in the USA
FSHW021046030821